I'm Not Crazy
I'm a Prophet

Second Edition

COLETTE TOACH

AMI BOOKSHOP

www.ami-bookshop.com

I'm Not Crazy – I'm a Prophet

Second Edition

ISBN-10: 1626640718
ISBN-13: 978-1-62664-071-9

1st Printing May 2014
2nd Edition May 2016

Published by **Apostolic Movement International, LLC**
E-mail Address: admin@ami-bookshop.com
Web Address: www.ami-bookshop.com

Contents

Prophets are...
Crazy!

Introduction – Prophets are Crazy!

Hello there. My name is Colette Toach and you have picked up this little book, because God has a message for you today.

Tell me something, what do you think defines a prophet?

Prophets are a dime a dozen these days. You find them now in many churches and everyone has this idea that the prophet is the guy standing up and giving the grand prophetic word each Sunday meeting.

Many imagine that he is the one running around after the meeting giving prophetic words to everyone.

Defining the Passion

What defines the prophet? It is their passion! It's their anger. It's their desire. It's their dream. It's their willingness to be crazy for the Lord!

It is the heart that they have for those that are hurting.

The prophet is the one that looks at the church and sees those being hurt and rejected. Their heart aches for those that knew the Lord, but then turned away because they were hurt by the church system.

The prophet also gets angry when he sees God's children being hurt and destroyed in the Church. He can't bear seeing the Holy Spirit wanting to move, but cannot because there are people preventing Him from doing it.

He cannot help himself! In fact, sometimes the passion is so strong that he starts to question himself and say, **"Lord what is wrong with me? I must be doing something wrong."**

The passion that the prophet has is what sets him apart. He has this crazy desire that everyone in the Church should belong and have a place. The prophet looks around and says, "Lord where does this person belong?"

Are You One of Those Crazies?

Are you one of those annoying types that keeps asking crazy questions such as,

> **"Why doesn't everyone have a place?"**

> **"Why are some people used in the church and others are not?"**

I am pretty sure that some of these questions have gotten you into a lot of trouble.

Be that as it may, you have a dream. A dream to see the Church be something it is not right now.

You want to come to church and see the Holy Spirit have His way. You want to throw out the programs and give God control.

Ok, to be fair, we can be a bit of a dramatic bunch and sometimes if we had our way, all structure would be thrown out the window. Thank the Lord for mentors and spiritual parents that can help you get some balance.

But hey – perhaps it was time that the church swung in the other direction! For years it has structured the Holy Spirit out of it, so perhaps some anointed chaos is just what we need.

The One Man Army

Of course the prophet is the over-eager soldier rushing headlong into the battlefield, sword swinging wildly giving all he has to defeat that enemy.

More often than not though after taking a few bashes to his head looks back and notices he is standing all alone in that battlefield, wondering what just happened.

The truth? The church has not caught up just yet. That is not to say it is not getting there! With the surge of prophetic ministries rising up, the Church is indeed changing. Perhaps it is because the prophets are maturing as well.

Instead of trying to take on the hordes of hell singlehandedly, you are stopping for a moment or two to plan your attack. There's something to be said for some good old prophetic maturity!

So it is good to delight in what makes you different and when you "have that down" you can stop for a moment to mature and reach back to the rest of the army out in the field to show them a better way.

Our Mistakes Make Way for Others

Perhaps the reason why the Lord allows the prophet to make so many mistakes is so that we can learn for others to avoid those mistakes.

You only need to fall on your face a few times to say with clear confidence, "Church of the Most High… trust me when I say – DO NOT go through that door!"

So all your mistakes were not a waste of time, they are learning tools for others to avoid the same pitfalls.

And so where you started out wanting to change the world, you discovered that the one who needed the most change is you. If you have come to that conclusion, then you are ready to start walking out the call that God has given to you.

How much do you want the Church to change? Well the change that the church goes through is quite the mathematic equation and it looks a little like this:

The change that the church will go through is equally matched to the amount of change that you are prepared to go through.

So are you crazy enough to become accountable? The Word says that the Church is laid on the foundation of the apostles and prophets. It also lists the prophets as the second highest ministry call.

So did you think then that you would be left scot free? If the church has to change, how much more do you have to be accountable?

As you let this sink in, you understand why you have gone the road you have. Why it has been harder than the roads of others. You now know why the trials are tougher and the fire hotter.

"Comfortable" is a Dirty Word

To whom much is given, must is also required. So yes, these trials and this fire does something to us. It makes us a little... odd in the eyes of others at times. The rest of the Church is allowed to slump every so often into complacency.

For one called to be a prophet – not so much! Complacency and "comfortable" are quite honestly dirty words in the mouth of the prophet!

Our comfort is two-fold though. Firstly, there is the comfort that the Lord Jesus made us a little crazy. He made us to stand out and to be accountable.

The second comfort is that you are not alone. You are just as odd as all the other prophets out there. In an age where the prophetic ministry is rising up in every denomination, you can rest assured that you are holding hands in the spirit with many other black sheep!

What You Want

You are just one of a new generation of spiritual soldiers who are crazy enough to want more in Church.

You dare to think to yourself...

"I want to walk into a meeting and see the Holy Spirit move. "

"I want to see people find their place."

"I want to see the bruised and broken healed."

"I want to see the lost restored."

"I want to see marriages and lives healed."

"I want to see believers with hard lives come into the presence of the Lord to receive healing."

"I want to see those bound by satan being set free."

Am I right? I know I am right! I am right because that is what defines a prophet.

It's not about how often you prophesy or about how many dreams you have. **God is not looking for how many gifts you can operate in.** God is looking for the heart of passion.

The Purpose of the Prophet

The prophet is called of God to introduce the Bride to Her Savior. He is called to make the church beautiful. Do you know how many believers walk through their Christian life not really knowing Jesus?

What is so easy for you - other believers do not have. Your ability to hear God's voice and your ability to enter into His presence through music is not the norm for everyone else. For many believers it feels like they are walking in a desert.

God has called you to take that believer by the hand and to teach them how to enter into a relationship with their loving Savior.

Imagine a church where every believer knows Jesus and can hear His voice for themselves. That is what the prophet is called to accomplish in the church.

You are not called to be a super hero and the only one that is able to hear from God. God is calling you to impart what you have to the church.

The Church Is Waiting for You!

If you think about the tough times you have faced, they do not compare to the change that God has called you to bring to His Church. There is a reason you have faced what you have!

The reason you have found yourself nailed to the cross again and again is because the church waits!

She waits for the prophets of God to rise up and birth the new apostolic move that God is doing. The Church waits for the prophets to rise up and release in the spirit what God wants to do.

Your Crazy is My Normal

Chapter 01 – Your Crazy is My Normal

Everyone glared at us from across the table. Tricked into a little "family gathering" Craig and I were caught in a situation we could not get out of.

We had announced our plans to pack our bags with our two toddlers and leave South Africa to join my parents in Mexico for the purpose of ministry.

"What are they thinking?"

"They are such irresponsible parents"

"What makes them think that they can make it in ministry?"

"They are just taking their kids away to starve in Mexico."

Everyone had an opinion and it was difficult to stand strong with so much opposition. It felt like all the hordes of hell were coming against us from circumstances, family and friends alike. However, no matter how hot the fire came, there was a conviction in both our hearts that would not budge.

No matter how crazy it sounded, we knew this move was of the Lord.

Well that was in 1998 and little did we know how one such move could transform our lives. Years later and we look at the international ministry that God has established and our two "toddlers" who are now young ladies and a vital part of our ministry team.

There are times in our lives as prophets where God calls on us to do crazy things, so trust me when I say that you are not alone.

Your Very First "Crazy."

No one ever forgets that familiar feeling of butterflies in your stomach the first time the Lord asks you to speak. Well when I first entered prophetic office, I did so with all the drama that follows a newbie prophet!

I was so excited about all the gifts and the revelations that God had given to me, that not a day passed by where I was not giving someone a prophetic word. Someone would write into the ministry asking how to subscribe to one of our mailing lists and I would respond with a prophetic word.

Ok... so things got a little out of hand. That is typical of me though. There are just no half measures and if anything is worth doing for the Lord – it is worth doing well!

Of course the enemy was only too eager to use that against me and my hunger to "tell everyone the truth" led more than once to speaking at the wrong time or speaking a revelation that was not from the Lord at all.

The Weight of Accountability

We have all been there! It is exciting to be used of the Lord, but it takes a few knocks down to realize the brevity of what He has called us to.

Speaking on His behalf is not a game or a fun pastime. It is about taking the lives of people into our hands.

Oh man, I was so overconfident! I was going to change the whole world singlehandedly. When the Lord opened the way for us to help out in a church in Europe, we were in boots and all.

I rearranged everything! I gave direction and stepped over leadership boundaries more than once. I just wanted so badly for everyone to know Jesus like I did. I wanted so much for everyone to have a place.

Well I had an abundance of good intention, but wisdom was not high on my agenda and instead of nurturing the Bride that Jesus loves so much, my excitement gave birth to some painful rejections.

Their Norm Was My Abnormal!

It turned out that not everyone was as ready as I was to turn the world upside down. In fact, they were quite happy with their little lives and simply wanted me to add the anointing to their norm.

The truth was though – their norm was abnormal to me. On the other hand, my norm was craziness to them. I felt like I was speaking Chinese in a German Church.

They should have understood my message, but they did not. So thought to myself, "These people need to change!"

Yes, true, they needed to change. However, God said to me, "You need to change!"

I hate it when He does that. Just when you think you have everything neatly sorted, He messes with the picture. Here I was, ready to change the world and the Lord said that first He needed to change me.

I had the fire. I had the passion. I had the revelation. What I lacked though was maturity and wisdom.

Do It With Style!

Walking in Godly wisdom took a little longer than receiving the prophetic gifts. I received the gifts of the spirit really easily and could interpret dreams and give prophetic words at the drop of a hat.

How to do it with style though – that took some practice. You see, I learned that being crazy was a good thing, but that for other people to "accept my crazy" I had to approach them differently.

I had to "dress my crazy up" in a way that they could receive it. I had to talk their language!

For the longest time I was convinced that people needed to see things my way. That was until the Lord gave me spiritual glasses and I saw the size of the beam in my eye. I was so ready to take out everyone else's splinter that I did not see I had a whole woodpile blocking my spiritual view.

I came to realize that it really did not matter if they saw things my way. It did not matter if they received my revelation and it did not matter if they judged me harshly.

All that mattered is that Jesus wanted the heart of His Bride and it was up to me to make that happen! My pride and my agenda?

That was the last matter of importance on God's list. At the top of His list, was His Bride and He wanted to know if I was willing to pay the price to make this happen.

Why We Are Different

The Lord set me apart for a purpose and He made me a little crazy so that I would see things that others did not. Since the day I was born, He geared me for something else.

There was a reason I was always on the outside looking in. God put me there! He put me there so that I could gain a new perspective of the world and church around me.

This perspective allowed me to see the broken and bruised. It opened my eyes to the flaws in the church and in my own heart alike.

Suddenly I realized that what the Lord had called me to be was not necessarily what He called the Church to be. I was a tool in His hand and this tool just so happened to be the oddest-looking one in the toolshed!

Keep Your Craziness

Perhaps you have experienced the same thing, but have come to the same wrong conclusions. You look at your craziness and the road you have traveled and think you need to "calm things down a bit."

Your fire and passion is not the problem here. It is just the way you are presenting it to people. So do not lose what defines you and makes you different. Rather be prepared to change and grow up.

When you get this concept, the work will be a quick one. The fire that the Lord has given us feels like an inferno sometimes. You do not know what to do with the passion and love you have inside.

However just "gushing it" over the next poor passerby is not the way to go. (Take my word of experience on that one.) Not everyone is ready for your great and mighty "gush."

So do not get offended if people do not understand. Rather ask the Lord for the right words in season to share it in a way that will reach them.

When Jesus spoke to Nicodemus, He "spoke his language." You see a distinct difference in the way that he spoke to him than he did to His disciples.

The Lord could reach everyone and that is where you will end up as well. First though, you need to see what makes you tick. Learn what makes you different and where to take it from here.

Not Everyone is Like You

The hardest part of the process is always being so different around other believers. You go from complaining about that difference to thinking that everyone should be like you.

What you need to realize is that you are different for a purpose and it is for you to help people find their own way, just like you found yours.

You know how hard it is to feel left out. Well in one way or another, every believer feels the same way as you do. Sure, not everyone is a prophet, but every believer has a calling.

Trust me, everyone feels like they are not fitting in. They feel like there is a purpose for their lives, but do not know where to fit.

That is where our own maturity comes into play. The purpose of our calling is not to try and make everyone into prophets, but to find out where they belong.

I can only flinch when I think back on how excited I was about being a prophet. For me it was "the call to have" and I saw prophets around me everywhere after that! I called everyone to death like the Lord called me to death.

I could not understand why the nicest people were avoiding me. I mean - what's not to love? Doesn't everyone love being chiseled, challenged, called to death and made to pay the price for the call?

It was a harsh reality to face – not everyone wanted to die! Are you kidding? Didn't they understand that it was the only way to resurrection?

It turns out that most believers are not so keen on the "flesh nailing, thorn piercing, spear thrusting" drama of prophetic training.

It turned out that each one had a unique call that had different trainings. It took me a while to figure that out and even today I cringe at the poor pastors I called to prophetic deaths.

A Little Sympathy for Those Pastors

I was so frustrated because they just did not "get it!" It turns out that I was the one who did not "get it." I am glad that today I can give Pastors a helping hand into their office without stabbing them in the side as they hang on the cross.

As I traveled on my journey I realized that there were those called to body ministries and some who were simply called to serve in the Church. What God had given to me was my unique call and it was for me to walk out – not for the entire church to walk out.

That changes things a bit doesn't it? It also brings a rest to who you are. You can accept who the Lord has made you to be and accept what the Lord has made others to be.

You can be your own kind of crazy and they can be theirs. Together though, we can be a Body that will shake this world!

Perhaps you can identify with some of what I have shared here and I hope that it has ignited the fire that is inside of you. The Lord has a place for you in His church. The travail you have gone through is worth it and what makes you so different is what sets you apart as something special.

So yeah, we are a crazy bunch, but right now the Church needs a little craziness. So let us join arms and rejoice in what makes us different. Then let us move on from there and bring the Church to a place of real change in the name of the Lord.

Prophets are... Different

Chapter 02 – Prophets are… Different

I am not much of an animal lover. It is strange because growing up, my mother actually loved dogs. I liked cats more but was just never much of a dog-person.

I ended up having four children though and you don't have to tell a child to love animals. Just as soon as they could talk and noticed a little kitty, doggy or ducky around, the nagging began. They wanted to have animals in their lives.

So what was I going to do now? I really didn't want a dog. They slobber, they shed, and they poop and chew up your favorite shoes.

However, my daughters discovered a way around my firm resolve, changing my mind every time.

They would say, "Oh, but Mommy, look! It's the little runt of the litter. The poor little thing is all alone and rejected. Nobody wants it…"

And so now you know how we ended up with our dogs. The one pup was found stranded on the street. There she was… looking like a little scrap. She was hungry, alone and stranded. Her puppy-dog eyes pleaded with me, "Please take me home. I am a very sad and lonely little dog."

Against my better judgment, I just couldn't help myself. What can I say? It was the runt. It was the little outcast that nobody wanted.

Well, to this day I can't resist a runt even though I am not a dog-person. You see, the little runt is the one that gets pushed around by all the other puppies. Not even its mother shows much interest.

The runt is usually the one that was born near the end and doesn't really have much of a hope for survival. In the wild, the runt often doesn't even make it. It dies before it comes to maturity.

Through these experiences though, I have found out that the runts that were rejected and thrown out, make the best dogs. They become the most loving and loyal companions. So much so that even I, this "un-doggy" person, really ended up loving each one. They found a way into my heart.

Hello There Mr. and Mrs. Runt!

As prophets, you and I are like the runts of the litter. I think that is why I have such a soft spot for the runt - the poor, scrawny, rejected, thrown-out little thing that nobody ever wanted.

I think the Lord has a soft spot for runts as well. He likes to take that little runt, hold it close and shower it with His love so that in the end that little runt turns out to be the most outstanding and wonderful creature.

> *1 Corinthians 1:27 But God has chosen the foolish things of the world to put to shame the wise, and God has chosen the weak things of the world to put to shame the things which are mighty.*

This passage has your name written all over it. It is in fact your confession as a prophet and I think a very fitting place to start this book.

So how about it? Shake it up and join me in saying,

> *But God has chosen* **[Your Name Here]** *as one of the foolish things of the world to put to shame the wise; and God has chosen* **[Your Name Here]** *because I am one of the weak things of the world chosen to put to shame the things that are mighty;*

In essence, that is what it is like to be a prophet. The reality is that you have never fitted in. You have always been the runt. You have always wanted to be like the other dogs but you never were. You never had the same desires as everybody else.

The secret here is that this is just the way God always wanted you to be! It is in the secret of your "runt-ness" that you will walk in His power. For when you are weak, then He is strong. When you are foolish, then He will be wise.

It is when we are the most weak and foolish that the Lord delights to step in and show the world exactly how wonderful He is. If this calling was a display of our natural strengths and abilities, then how would that glorify God?

Colette Toach

If you stood up in all your carefully nurtured abilities, how would you say, "Look at Jesus in me." When in reality you are saying, "Look how fantastic I am?"

As a prophet there is no place for a boast in yourself. If you even try for a moment, you can be sure to feel your tender faced pressed up hard against a cold, stonewall. So if you are tired of sand in your eyes and brick in your teeth, then face the facts.

Accept the "runt" in you that God has called and chosen. When you do, you will discover the hidden power of Jesus.

What Makes You Different?

In this first Chapter, we will look at what makes you different as a prophet. Hopefully by the end of it you are so happy about those differences that you are ready to take them and rise up.

Why are you, little runt, so different to the other big dogs "out there"?

1. You See Things Differently

If you are a prophet, you have this nasty habit of going to a church and seeing all the things that are wrong there right away. Well, that doesn't make you very popular, does it?

Well it might not make you popular, but it sure makes you a prophet! It makes you different and it is something

God put inside of you. He has given you the ability to see things differently.

You cannot understand why no one else notices that God's people are being trodden all over in the church. You notice when the one person with true potential is looked over for someone who has more talent and no anointing.

You are a little like me... you keep noticing the runts and wishing you could heal and reach out to them.

When something does not line up with the Word of God it irritates you. When the Holy Spirit is told to sit in the back row because He had the nerve to show up before the announcements, you want to march yourself, your family and everyone else in the church right out the door!

So yes, maybe you are like a little runt that's constantly annoying people but praise the Lord, because it is exactly what you are meant to be.

Seeing things differently is a quality that defines you as a prophet. So stop wishing that you were like everybody else and realize that because you see things differently you have a greater potential to bring change to the body of Christ.

2. You Know the Language of the Spirit

"Get your head out of the clouds!"

"You are just over-spiritualizing everything"

"Can't you just be normal? Why are you so religious?"

"Why can't we just have 'fun' instead of praying?"

Do any of these phrases sound familiar to you? Not to worry though, because there is a reason why you have this crazy flaw of being so "spiritual." It is because the Lord needs you to think in pictures.

> *Numbers 12:6 Then He said, Hear now My words: If there is a prophet among you, I, the Lord, make Myself known to him in a vision; I speak to him in a dream.*

You are meant to see things in types and shadows, because this is the language of the spirit.

Perhaps you were one of those kids that always had their nose in a fantasy novel growing up. Maybe you preferred watching movies and were into the fantasy stuff.

In any case, you likely sat in your daydream world for hours, dreaming up things and always thinking in pictures.

What it said of you that you were more often "in the clouds" than in reality? If so, then you have a reason for a praise party. It may make you different but once again it is something that defines your prophetic calling.

As a prophet, you are meant to think in pictures!

Perhaps that made you a bit weird growing up. Perhaps you were likely not much of the studious type and preferred to read a fantasy book or do something that encouraged you to use your imagination.

Maybe you were very creative and loved developing that side of you. I want to reassure you here that this is a good thing. In fact, it is one of the signs of the prophetic calling.

It's Ok to Be the Dreamer

There is no doubt that you faced pressures to conform to everyone else. Being allegorical and having your head in the clouds has probably caused you more trouble than you can count.

For me, it gave me a royal pain up the side of my head… literally! I was walking home from school and entertaining, once again, my flamboyant daydream world.

My feet were leading me home faithfully and in my mind I was soaring high above in the clouds, escaping all the problems I had faced that day.

My dreamy state was brought to a sudden and confused stop as my tender little head connected with an unforgiving streetlight pole. My head echoed with the sound of a mighty "gong" and a flash of pain spread across my cheek like fireworks.

That hardly hurt compared to the reality. Next to me a burst of laughter erupted as a group of peers guffawed at my dilemma. I guess to be fair it must have looked pretty strange.

The movie in my mind of walking right into a pole that was clearly in the middle of my path played over in my thoughts all the way home.

So yes, our idealistic view of what the Church should look like and the tendency to drift off into allegorical thinking can get you into trouble. However, it is also the source of the revelation that sets you apart.

Even Jesus Himself, when He stood up to preach, spoke in parables. He spoke in pictures and told stories all the time.

You have all this potential inside of you. It is like a bomb that is waiting to go off. However, you have always kept it down because you thought that being different as you are was just more trouble than it was worth.

So I want to take some of that pressure off you. You don't have to be all left-brained and be a thinker. Realize that God has made you to be a dreamer.

You have to speak the mind of Christ and not your own and that will happen through your spirit.

Don't be afraid then to let your difference stand out. In fact, develop it because that is a requirement for you as a prophet.

3. Me and My Big Mouth!

Another thing that makes you very different (I don't even have to be a prophet to say this) is that you say things you should not.

You open that big mouth of yours and you end up saying a whole bunch of things you shouldn't be saying. You tend to upset people.

Hot or Cold? Lukewarm Gets "the Boot"

Your mouth runs ahead of your head because you see things in black and white. There is no in between with you. The Church is either cold or hot – lukewarm has no place.

> *Revelation 3:16 So then, because you are lukewarm, and neither cold nor hot, I will vomit you out of My mouth.*

This is a passage that you live by as a prophet and rightly so. It stems from a fire kindled in the Throne room of God Himself.

You see things in the body of Christ that are not right but you do not stop there. You make this little mistake... you open your big mouth and express those views!

How many times has that gotten you into trouble? Take me aside and whisper an answer to me, "How many churches has that gotten you kicked out of?"

Did you think you were the only one that got kicked out of a church because of your big mouth? Welcome to the club! Most prophets I know have been there at one time or another.

You faced rejection and experienced the "right boot of fellowship" up close and personal.

You are just a little runt with a big mouth that says things that you shouldn't. Well, praise the Lord for that!

That's what makes you different. It's what defines you and sets you apart. It is exactly what God wants you to be.

Perhaps after one too many uncomfortable "invitations to explore other church options" you thought that it might be better for you to shut up and try to be like everybody else. To a certain extent you are right.

You have to learn when it is wise for you to remain silent and when you need to open that big mouth of yours and say something.

Don't worry though because that is why you are reading this. I will help you out with that problem. I will show you when you should and shouldn't be speaking.

However, don't let this be a reason for you to stop noticing things altogether. Don't let this discourage you from seeing things in black and white. Don't give up on your passion because of this.

Unfortunately, though, instead of allowing that pressure to let your fire come out even more strongly, you have allowed it to do the opposite. You have allowed your passion to dwindle.

Listen, you are meant to be different. It is because of all the differences we have looked at so far, that you are going to be able to fulfill your prophetic mandate. You need these differences just like a potter needs a wheel on which to shape the clay.

Until you learn to develop those differences you won't be able to stand up in the fullness of what God has for you.

Praise the Lord and Burn Brightly

So thank the Lord for it! It doesn't matter that you say things that you shouldn't say because at least you have the courage to do so. The body of Christ needs that. The Church needs people like you, with the courage to say what needs to be said, regardless of the rejection you might face because of it.

If you stick to your guns, then at least we will have one prophet that stands up and says the truth while everybody else is in deception!

We need more prophets in the body of Christ who have the courage to say the things they "shouldn't" because there are a lot of people who are saying things that are leading God's people astray.

So, you and I need to get in there and rock the boat. Maybe we are a couple of runts howling at the moon at midnight, but you know what, we will bring change to the body of Christ. At the end of the day isn't that what it is all about?

So your difference has gotten you into trouble sometimes. If you are honest, you know that you were out of line at times.

Ok, so maybe it would have been better for you to keep your yap shut that one time when you said "that thing" to "that pastor" in front of everybody.

It was perhaps a stupid thing to do, but that does not mean you have to stay there or allow it to cripple your calling.

The point I want to make here is that no matter what; do not allow the experiences you have had to take your courage away. Don't let these things snuff out the fire that burns inside of you.

You need that fire, because without it, you are not going to accomplish your mandate. You need to think and see things differently in order for you to accomplish it. So don't be afraid to let all those differences come out even more strongly than before.

4. Prayer – the Very Breath of God!

Why is it that most believers think of prayer as such a chore?

Am I the only one who has experienced this? You announce a prayer meeting and only a few (if any) show up? The ones that show up are usually all the prophetic types. They love to pray! Everybody else would prefer to go to a praise party or something that feels more exciting.

Everybody is always looking for the next fun thing to do. Nobody wants to stop to spend time in prayer. It is just not exciting to them. For the prophets however, it is a strong passion.

Many say, "Oh, I really have to try and make time for prayer". To the prophet though it is not just about prayer, it means talking to the Lord and building a relationship with Him.

Watching the Seconds Tick By...

When I was a child I lived with my grandparents for a few months. They had a scheduled prayer meeting every morning with the family at seven o'clock.

Seven was way too early for me to get spiritual at that time. You may as well be getting up in the middle of the night as far as I was concerned. It was especially difficult in winter when it was so cold and dark.

Well, here we were at seven in the morning and it was time to pray.

To you that may sound wonderful – a nice little family prayer time. How nice. Yeah right! Perhaps in a make-believe world. In reality, it was Monday morning and I was tired, cold and still had to go to school.

And so the barely audible prayers would begin. "Thank you Lord for this day. I thank you that I will have a good day at school. Thank you that you will bring us home safely again… amen."

I would watch the old cuckoo clock on the wall as each second echoed loudly through the silent room. It felt like an eternity between each "tick" and "tock" however at exactly five minutes past seven we would all be finished with our prayers and off to school.

You know, that really is not my idea of prayer. I am pretty sure it is not yours either, but unfortunately, this is how many other believers see it.

When you are all excited and say to someone, "I am going to pray", they have flashbacks of their own versions of that cuckoo clock in their head, ticking in slow motion as they try not to nod off.

When you have not been taught about the job of prayer it loses it passion and becomes a chore. They think, "Well, it's the right thing to do but the Lord is probably not listening anyway. "

As a prophet, you definitely don't see it like that. You have come to understand the hidden secret of prayer. You know that praying is just another word for "love affair with Jesus." And so to pray for you is to hide away and be swept into another world

It means sitting on the throne and speaking out decrees. It means hearing the Lord whisper His secrets in your ear.

Is it no surprise that prophets will find any chance that they get to hide away with the Lord? You pray on your way to work. You pray while you cook. You pray in the bathtub (still my favorite place to get the most profound revelations!).

You have tapped into a secret that most believers have not and instead of allowing it to bring separation, you should be pouring out some of that fire! When you can teach others to experience the same things that you do when you are alone with the Lord, you will transform the Church.

Your "difference" is like the simple atom. Alone, it does not seem like much, but put it in the right circumstances and you have the potential for a bomb that is devastating!

I will end this section with a little prayer incident that explains a little about how different we are as prophets.

We had just arrived in Mexico from South Africa and it was Craig's first time to drive in a foreign country. Now what made matters a bit nerve wrecking is that in South Africa we drive on the opposite side of the road – British style.

The huge freeways here made him nervous and he was watching every move he made on the road.

Sitting in the passenger seat I was not really thinking about his dilemma, but in true "prophet fashion" figured that now was a good time as any to pray.

So while he gripped his steering wheel with determination, I sat next to him and just spoke in tongues quietly the whole way.

The trip was a good 40 minutes long and next to the rise and fall of my voice as I prayed, the car was silent. The hum of the tires on the road seemed to support my prayer as we drove on.

Finally, we reached our destination and Craig managed to make his way into a parking space. He had just survived his first international driving experience.

I felt refreshed after a good time of prayer, unaware that my incessant praying all the way had been viewed as something completely different by Craig.

He turned the engine off and with his hand still clutching the steering wheel, he looked at me sheepishly and said, "Love, was my driving really that bad?"

Prophet, passion and prayer all go hand in hand! Craig and I have since learned to communicate better and make sure that during our long trips, that we pray... together!

5. You Are an Anointing Junkie

We have an inside joke in our ministry. In our first prophetic school (launched in 1999) we had an application that had a question that most prophets answered the same way.

The question was: If there is anything that you could change in the Church, what would it be?

The very surprising common answer in various wording boiled down to, "Remove the chairs so that God's people can worship the Lord with abandon!"

You see, when prophets praise, you need to get yourself out of the way. They want to raise their hands, they want to shout and dance. They want to express themselves without holding back.

Unfortunately, it is not always acceptable because depending on your denomination there seems to be an unspoken law in many churches that says,

"You can clap. That's okay. Perhaps you can shuffle a bit and it may even be okay to raise your hands a bit. As soon as it goes anywhere outside of that though, people get uncomfortable."

You are in a praise meeting and the power comes down. What is a prophet to do? The only thing a prophet can do! They begin to praise God with all their might.

That is when you will find people moving away from you. They start looking at you funny and have the nerve to feel embarrassed for you.

"There goes the little runt doing that "thing" again...."

We know the truth though. We know that it is in praise and worship that you bring the glory of God down!

You know the power that Jehoshaphat discovered in this passage.

> *2 Chronicles 20:21 After consulting the people, Jehoshaphat appointed men to sing to the LORD and to praise him for the splendor of his holiness as they went out at the head of the army, saying: 'Give thanks to the LORD, for his love endures forever.' 22 As they began to sing and praise, the LORD set ambushes against the men of Ammon and Moab and Mount Seir who were invading Judah, and they were defeated. (NIV)*

Jehoshaphat was an anointing junkie too because he knew the power of praise. By praising the Lord, not only will you sense His presence, but also it is where you see things happen.

That is why it is my firm belief that prophets should lead the praise and worship team in the Church. Praise and worship runs in their veins. They might not have the talent, but they sure have the passion for it.

It is not seen often enough in the Church though. Usually the prophet is the one handling the projector and song sheets while everybody else worships. The prophet is the one who will eventually stand at the very back of the church, dancing and praising the Lord because nobody else wants to stand next to him.

They make too much noise. They rock the boat and make a fuss... that crazy little runt! What is that runt up to now? This runt is praising the Lord! It sets you apart.

Join the Flock of Black Sheep

So you are the black sheep and don't fit in. That's okay, because God didn't mean for you to fit in. Perhaps you rock the boat and upset people but we will work on that. I will teach you how avoid upsetting people all the time.

I will show you how to just get in there and make a fuss sometimes, because you can't avoid it altogether. Rocking the boat is part of your call.

It is a simple fact that you will say things others don't want to hear and expose things they don't want to see.

Welcome - this is normal here in this flock of black sheep. If you are called to be a prophet, you welcome the challenge. You want people to change you.

So Let me "Give It to You Straight"

You grew up being different but wanted to fit in with the rest of the kids at school. You wanted to fit in with your neighbors, your siblings and with all your family but you never did.

Your whole life you tried hard to be normal and to be one of the popular kids. You always fell short though. Well, it is because you were meant to fall short.

Allow me to let you in on another secret.

Think about the people that really make it in this world - why do you think they are so popular?

It is not because they are so normal. In fact, the exact opposite is true. They are admired because they are so different and because they have confidence and pride in their difference. They are not afraid to boast in their difference.

Think of anybody that stands out to you as you look through your life. Look at the people around you that are popular and always have friends.

They are the trendsetters, aren't they? They are the ones that will wear something different just to make a point. They will drive something different just to make a point.

You see, they boast in their difference and as a result, people are drawn to that like moths to a flame. There is something inside of us that attracts us to something different.

However, when you are not confident in that difference, you will just be rejected. When you are confident in your difference, it draws people to you.

It is important that you adapt this attitude especially for ministry. If you want people to start receiving from you, you will have to come to a point of just relaxing in your difference.

Be bold, confident and full of joy about what makes you different. If you can do that, then you will be like a light that draws moths to a flame. You will be like an explosion in the Church that others will come to be warmed up by.

So perhaps you are the little runt of the litter. However, you are the most prized possession out of the whole lot that the Lord has picked out, held close and raised up to be something magnificent in the body of Christ.

A Definition of the Prophet

Chapter 03 – A Definition of the Prophet

At the end of the day, there is no better way for me to "let go" than to tuck myself neatly away into my kitchen.

After a day of pouring out in ministry, getting revelation and handling the hundred other loads of the ministry - tackling a block of meat and chopping an onion until I cry is a nice respite from everything else.

Perhaps I feel this way because cooking is such a normal thing to do. Mostly though it is because I love the creativity of it! I do not need to be an apostle to cook... I can just be "me" and create something fun that takes care of my family.

And so, cooking is something I enjoy to do. It breaks me out of my day and reminds me that my children still need their "mom" for the simple things in life.

My husband, ever keen to maintain this excitement in me, was only too happy to buy me all the nice pots and pans I needed for the craft!

He did not skimp on nice knives either, because we all know that at the end of the day... a way to a man's heart is to his stomach. (For you ladies out there... as traditional as this sounds... it still holds true!)

The most interesting thing though, is that in all the years that I have put my heart into cooking, I have never had anybody sit down, taste my food to say,

"Wow, these are such great pots and pans that you used for this food."

I could not imagine a greater insult!

"You mean to say my food is as good as my pot?! That is the last time I make dinner for you Mister!"

The Prophetic Pot

As strange as this illustration may sound, this is pretty much what is happening in the prophetic ministry in the Church right now.

A prophet stands up to speak and instead of the Church saying, "Wow, I can really see how they are maturing the body of Christ" they say, "Wow! Did you hear that prophetic word? That was the greatest pot I ever heard!"

So what I would like to do here is to separate the myth from the reality of what the prophetic is about.

Unfortunately, in many places and maybe even in your own life, you look at the prophetic ministry as pots and pans - as the tools you use.

You judge yourself by the way you prophesy or bring the words of wisdom and knowledge.

You think that if you can use nice and expensive pots and pans that this makes you into a good cook. That is not necessarily true. In fact, I have seen some chefs using the worst pots make the most delicious meals.

So What Defines a Prophet?

Why is this? It is because it is not about the tools that you use but rather what you present at the end of the day. It is all about the end picture.

And so it is not about how well you prophesy or even how many of the gifts of the spirit you flow in that makes you into a prophet, but it is about what you produce when you use those tools that makes you dish up something great for the Church!

What makes me a good cook is not my pots and pans but it is my creativity and the things that motivate me.

What makes a prophet is what burns in him. What defines him is what he wants to do in the body of Christ and the impact he makes on it.

If I am in a group and want to find out who the prophet is, do you know what I ask? I ask this simple question, "Tell me, what burns in you? If you could do absolutely anything you want for the Lord, what would it be?"

You say, "Well, that's a strange question. Shouldn't it be obvious that somebody is a prophet if they prophesy all the time?"

It is not so. What answer do you think I am looking for when I ask somebody that question? Well, let me tell you what the prophet will say.

They will say, "You know, it really burns in me to set the captives free in the body of Christ. I see so many believers backslidden and broken, I would just like to reach in and heal them. I just want to see them restored. I also see so many Christians torn down from the pulpit that I would like to see them built up.

I want to see them in their rightful place in the Church. I would like to see the Holy Spirit really having free reign in the meetings without restriction."

When I hear that sort of answer I say, "Hello prophet!"

What?! You're a Prophet and You Don't Prophesy?!

Even if it turns out that this person can't prophesy or doesn't receive any dreams, I will still recognize their prophetic calling.

Come again?

Well, if I only have one pot, does that mean that I am not a cook anymore?

It will make my job a little harder, but it doesn't mean that I can't cook. And so it is the same with the prophet. Just because you don't function in all of the gifts doesn't mean that you are not called to be a prophet. It just indicates that you are a little restricted but it doesn't mean that you are not called.

On the other hand, I knew someone who had such fancy kitchen equipment. They had so many pots and pans but they didn't cook.

Does that make them a chef? Does it mean that just because they own every kitchen tool under the sun they are suddenly a great chef…?

Once again, you see it is all about what you do with those tools that matters. It is what you do with the gifts that sets you apart and not the gifts themselves.

Gifts vs. Calling

So let me issue a little challenge to you here. I want you to take a look at the people you meet and forget about the gifts they operate in.

Let me remind you that every single believer has the ability to flow in the gifts. Apostle Paul never said that the gift of prophecy was only for the prophets. In fact, he said, "…so that you may ALL prophesy." Every single believer has the ability to flow in all of the spiritual gifts.

So now that we made that clear, what is it that sets the prophet apart then? It is how he matures the body of Christ through his gifts.

Consider *Ephesians 4:11-12 And He Himself gave some to be apostles, some prophets, some evangelists, and some pastors and teachers, for the equipping of the saints for the work of ministry, for the edifying of the body of Christ,*

It doesn't say here that it is about prophesying prophetic words, about the dreaming of dreams or the seeing of visions. Paul clearly says that it is all about the maturing of the saints and the building up of the Body.

Very simply put, the prophet is called to mature the body of Christ by taking every believer to a place where they know the Lord Jesus in an intimate way.

The Sought After Prophetic Word

There are so many believers in the Church who want prophetic words. You know why they want them?

It is because they want to hear from the Lord. They are much like a man who is completely starved.

So you go and get him a fish. However, tomorrow he is hungry again and asks you to feed him again.

Now how much better would it be to get that man a boat, give him a fishing rod and teach him how to fish so he can catch his own fish every day? Which way do you think is really benefiting him?

It is the same in the prophetic ministry. Everybody wants to get a prophetic word because they are hungry to hear from the Lord.

So what will you do about it? Will you keep dishing out the prophetic words just so they come back to you tomorrow because they are hungry again?

A prophetic word is a rhema word for the now. It is not like a teaching. I think the teachers sometimes have it a little easier because they can just rely on teaching that can be taught again and again.

However, a prophetic word can't be given again and again. It is like manna – you eat it today and tomorrow it is full of worms and doesn't mean anything anymore.

You know, perhaps in time it may mean something to you again, but generally speaking when you receive a word from the Lord or stumble across a prophetic word, it ministers to you right then and there.

Let me tell you a little secret - there are very few words that can really stand the test of time. There may be some, but in general when it is a word of knowledge or wisdom at the prophetic ministry level, it is just for the "now".

So if you keep giving the prophetic words, believers will be excited that they are hearing the voice of the Lord. However, tomorrow they will be feeling down again because life is tough... it's a reality! Well, the first thing they say is. "Well, let me go back to the prophet again!"

And so you keep handing out the fishes instead of teaching the man how to fish for himself.

As a prophet your function is not to hand out prophetic words. Your prophetic words are meant to draw them closer to the Lord to teach them about Him.

It is for you to take them under your wing and teach them how to hear from the Lord for themselves.

Now You're Cooking!

You see, now you are cooking! Now you are using the pots and pans in the right place. The time you will really find the prophetic gifts come in handy is when you are doing prophetic counseling.

In this setting you will get revelation about people's problems and you can minister to their hurts. Then you can lay hands on them and speak healing and bring change to their lives.

You see now you are cooking... Now you are fulfilling the prophetic function and are operating in your calling.

So what are you really looking for when we are talking about a prophet? What is the Lord looking for? He is looking for that fire.

Find Your "Star Quality"

Just like the creative flair sets a chef apart, so does that fire set the prophet apart and so that is what you are looking for.

You are looking for a prophet that has a desire to bring change to the body of Christ.

A prophet is somebody who wants to do something different. He is somebody who wants to take a believer and see them rise up in maturity.

You can't judge a prophet by the gifts he has. However, you can judge him by the fruit – by the plate of food he presents to you. What has he given you to eat, what do you go home with?

Do you go home with a bit of fluff in your head or do you go home having had an experience with the Lord? Do you go home with a principle, an ability to touch God again and again for yourself?

This is how you are bringing the body of Christ to maturity! You need to feed them so they can go home with something solid without having to come back next week empty handed.

A prophet is defined by the job that he does not by the tools that he does it with. Sure, the tools make your job a whole lot easier, but they don't define your job.

In fact, you should be handing those tools out to the rest of the body of Christ and teaching them how to use them for themselves. You should teach them to grow up a bit and to function in the gift of discerning of spirits so that they can discern what's of God and what is not.

Using the Gifts – Create a Masterpiece!

It is great that you have started to function in the gifts and I certainly want to encourage that in you. I want you to flow in all the gifts of the spirit and to really learn how to use your tools.

It would be dumb of a chef to use just one pot. In the same way I encourage you to use all of the gifts that are available to you. However, I want you to understand clearly that this is not what defines you as a prophet.

What defines you is the fire that burns inside of you and your desire to see the body of Christ equipped just like it says in Ephesians 4.

You are called to equip the saints, to mature man and to bring him to a place of maturity, to a place where he is not the same as he was before. That is your function in the body of Christ. Are you beginning to see the picture clearly?

I know I am belaboring this point a bit but I am just really seeing so much abuse of this in the body of Christ. Everybody that can prophesy and flow in the gifts is a labeled a prophet. No! That is just like saying that anybody who bought a bunch of pots is a good cook....

Sure, you can make bacon and eggs, but you know what, there is a little bit more to cooking than that.

It is the same with the prophetic. Sure, you can flow in the gift of the word of knowledge, but there is much more to the prophetic than that. It is more than just throwing out a few words and sounding and looking good.

Your Accountability

Being a prophet means to take on the responsibility and bring change to the body of Christ. It means to mature believers and not just to throw out any old words that they could get anywhere else also.

You are called to teach believers how to hear from God for themselves so that they can journal and get prophetic words every day of their lives. When you do that, then you are maturing the body of Christ. In doing this you are bringing change.

As a prophet, this sort of thing burns in you. You are saying, "yeah, yeah," to this! You are saying, "I am sick of the fluff. I am sick of the flakiness."

Perhaps you have even been put off by some of the drama you see in the Church. Perhaps you have looked at the prophetic movement and seen some of the others and then thought to yourself, "I'd rather not be a prophet, thank you."

Well, I don't blame you. You know, if that is what it means to be a prophet, I wouldn't want to be one either. So thank the Lord that's not what it means to be a prophet.

The Lord has something greater for you. Be encouraged now to start seeing the picture clearly. You can also refer to the ten signs of the prophetic calling that we cover in the *Practical Prophetic Ministry* book in the first few chapters. When you go through those signs you will also see clearly that your calling is truly not based on the gifts.

In fact, it is based on the motivations of your heart and the things that you have gone through. I want you to understand this well, because it is great that you can understand and identify the calling in your life, but what about identifying it in others?

Can you spot other prophets? Can you see the prophetic child, because of the things that burn in them?

So Tell Me Prophet – What's So Special About You?

So tell me? What is a prophet? What defines a prophet?

What defines you is what burns in your heart, and that is to see change in the body of Christ, to see believers coming into a relationship with the Lord and to see them rising up in authority over the problems in their lives! You are passionate about seeing believers take authority over satan in their lives.

There is nothing more exciting that taking the time to teach somebody those principles and seeing them rise up as they apply them. You as a prophet, get to have your hand in this so this change takes place.

You and I we are limited in what we can do. No matter how much exposure we have, we can only reach so many people. We can only give so many prophetic words and can only give so many directions.

However, if we can teach others how to use the tools they have and if we can teach them how to mature and rise up, in turn they can teach others and we will have a greater effect on the body of Christ in this way. We will continuously duplicate ourselves. In this way we will bring the body of Christ to that place of maturity!

So what's cooking in your kitchen? What are you dishing out? Maybe you even have some good tools and maybe you don't. At the end of the day, what are you really accomplishing in your prophetic calling?

You are the only one that will be able to judge that!

The Face-to-Face Relationship With Jesus

Chapter 04 – The Face-to-Face Relationship With Jesus

Introduction – It All Starts With a Relationship

Being an amiable, my husband Craig knows everybody and everybody knows him. I remember when we were first dating, it didn't matter what part of town we went to, it was almost a given that he would bump into somebody he knew.

They would say, "Hey Craig! How's it going?"

I would stand there next to him feeling uncomfortable and unsure of how to handle this situation as the "new girlfriend".

And so most times he would introduce me to them. Other times, however, he didn't. Those were usually the times when he forgot the person's name and was too embarrassed to proceed.

Over the years, nothing much has changed. We can still go anywhere in town and there will be people that recognize him and he recognizes them. We pump gas and the attendant breaks out in a big smile to see him again.

The security guard at the local store makes a special effort to give him a toothless grin and hello when he sees us driving up.

So if there is anybody you would like to meet there is a good chance that if you get a hold of Craig, he can organize it. He knows them in some way from some place and so they got a relationship.

When I look at this, I see the perfect picture of what the prophet is meant to be in the body of Christ. So far we have covered a lot about what the prophet does.

So now, let me ask you this one question: What is the most important thing you have to accomplish in your training to call yourself a prophet?

The answer is a face-to-face relationship with Jesus. You see, when you have a face-to-face relationship with Jesus and He is somebody you know closely, you can then fulfill your mandate as a prophet. A vital part of that mandate is to introduce Him to the body of Christ.

Time to Grow Up!

We have already looked a bit at the maturity of the prophet and what it takes to mature the body of Christ. We saw how the Lord gave the Fivefold Ministry to the Church for the maturing of the saints.

Let's go a little bit deeper now and look at what it really means to mature the saints. Does it mean that everybody has to fast and pray? I don't think so.

So then, how can you fulfill your mandate as a prophet if you don't really know what it means to mature the saints?

Let me make it easy for you. The answer to this is found in a powerful and familiar passage of Scripture. Take note and memorize this passage. It is one of my favorites.

> *1 Corinthians 13:10 But when that which is perfect has come, then that which is in part will be done away.*
> *11 When I was a child, I spoke as a child, I understood as a child, I thought as a child; but when I became a man, I put away childish things.*
> *12 For now we see in a mirror, dimly, but then face to face. Now I know in part, but then I shall know just as I also am known.*

Apostle Paul goes on to even say that there will be visions and there will be all the gifts of the spirit. However, after all that he says "Let me show you a higher way. There is a better and greater way! There is something more magnificent and that is the power of love!"

When you have that face-to-face relationship with Jesus and you come into that love walk with Him, the visions go away, the prophecies go away and you enter into a higher dimension.

"You mean to tell me that giving prophetic words is not the beginning and the end of prophetic ministry?!"

"Oh man! How will I survive? How can I call myself a prophet?"

Take it easy. Slow down and take a deep breath… I am here to show you an even more exciting way.

You Ain't No Michael Jackson

Have you been looking for that higher realm of spirituality? This is where you will find it. People think, if they want to become more spiritual that this means that they must read the Word more, speak in tongues more and fast through more.

Let me burst that bubble for you quickly so that we can get on with it. This is not the way to impress the Lord.

In Mexico it is not uncommon to see a performer at the traffic lights trying to get your attention with the hopes that you will put something into his donation tin. The best I ever saw was a 60-year-old man doing a perfect impersonation of Michael Jackson's "Thriller" moves.

He had the moonwalk down pat. The tilted hat finished it off with his cool white suit and glove. Boy could he swing his booty around that tarmac. Even if he did not have all his teeth, his face wrinkled by the harsh sun was set in a permanent grin, which added to the charm.

You could give him 100 points for trying! However, no matter how much he slid across that intersection, he would never be Michael Jackson. No amount of effort would make that happen for him.

How often though do we think that to become something for the Lord, we need to put on a good show?

There is a better way to get the Lord's attention than by pulling all the moves that we think will impress Him.

If you want to enter into a higher realm of spirituality, if you want to become a spiritual giant, the secret is in 1 Corinthians 13. I want you to go read that Chapter and let it sink into your spirit until you get the rhema word of God enlightening and shaking you.

You want that spiritual maturity? Do you want to become the mighty warrior that you are not right now?

You will get it in a face-to-face relationship with Jesus. You will become that warrior when you come to the point where you know as you are known - in other words when you know Him as He knows you.

When you come to that place then He is more real to you than anybody else in this world... then you would have reached that higher level.

It's Really Simple

It starts with a simple friendship. It is just like in the illustration I shared at the beginning, of my husband Craig. He was just so open to have friendships with people. That is exactly where it all begins.

I don't know what kind of friends you have but the kind of friends I have are the kind you have fun with!

They are the ones I can share my heart with and take anywhere with me! Now those are some real friends.

Those are the ones that you develop the closest bonds for.

If you have to perform for a friend, if you have to do things to impress them, then I am sorry to say this, but they are not a real friend.

The Lord Jesus – Your Very Best Friend!

The Lord Jesus is one of the best friends you could ever have in this world. You don't have to perform for Him to make Him want to be with you and have a relationship with you. So, if you want to make it through prophetic training, this is your starting point.

Sure, the gifts are there also however, consider that your dating phase. How to prophesy, using your Urim and Thummim, journaling... all these things help you get familiar with the Lord, but all the gifts in the world are not enough.

I am so sad to see so many prophets stopping right there. They say, "Oh, I can prophesy! I can have dreams and visions!"

You're not moonwalking yet! You just got started. There is a whole new dimension that you are about to step into.

Flowing in the gifts of the spirit is great but it is just the starting point. It is just dating, not even good honeymoon yet...

The real crux of your prophetic ministry lies in your face-to-face relationship with Jesus! From there you can go from height to height, from maturity to maturity.

Then, when you are at that place and only when you are there, are you ready to fulfill your mandate as a prophet to the Church universal. You can go around prophesying to everybody and giving them grand revelations, but you are not fulfilling your mandate.

Your mandate as a prophet is to introduce the Bride to the groom. If you don't know the groom, then you will have a real problem introducing Him...

Remember, "What's His Name?"

Just like when Craig and I came to somebody whose name he couldn't remember, he couldn't introduce us, could he? Nope, instead he left his girlfriend standing there with a fixed, pained smile on my face and a look in my eyes that said, "You did NOT just do that to me again!"

How many prophets do we see in the body of Christ today who can't introduce the bride to the groom?!

They can't even hear the voice of God for themselves. They have to go find another prophet to prophesy over them...

If you are going to complete your training and really do the things that God has called you to do it is time to put away childish things and to change your mindset - it is time to bring the body of Christ to maturity!

So it is time that you come to that place of maturity for yourself! The only time when we will see real change in the Church is when every single believer can enter into a relationship with Jesus for themselves - where every single believer can hear the voice of God for themselves and are not reliant on the prophet. It is your job as a prophet to make that happen!

Howdy Prophet! Great to See You!

When you are doing that you are being a prophet! Will people recognize you by the things you have done for them in their lives or by the grand prophetic words you gave?

When you leave a place, what would you have left behind that the people can hold onto? Just a few words from the Lord or have you given them the Lord Jesus Himself in their midst?

How are the prophets going to come to a place to judge? Apostle Paul says that the prophets are subject to the prophets. So how are you going to come to that place?

"You need to know the Word of God", you say? Yes, of course. It is a great place to start. It is your foundation and I preach about that plenty in our prophetic school. However, you need to be able to recognize His voice through the Word and through the Spirit.

Hmm, He Said That Did He?

There is one way that I have really learned to perfect that in my marriage. I have kids... I am sure you know it well. Kids are the same around the world. They will come to me and say, "Hey Mommy - Daddy said this and this."

I know my husband well so I say, "Did he really?"

They reply, "Yeah, Dad said it was okay. He said we could go now to play. He said we didn't have to finish our chores."

I am sitting there thinking that this really doesn't sound like my husband!

So I get a hold of him and I say, "Hey Craig, did you tell the kids that they could go and play right now?"

And he says, "No. That is not what I said!"

You know how kids are. They will try it more than once. You see - I know my husband. I know his voice and I know how he thinks. I know what decisions he is going to make and that's why nobody can come to me and say, "Craig said this and this!" I will know right away whether they are talking garbage or not.

Well, do you have that kind of relationship with the Lord Jesus where a prophet can stand up and say, "Thus says the Lord..." and you because you know the Lord you know that this is not what he sounds like?

In many of our prophetic courses we ask our students to submit their journals as part of their practical projects. When we look at those journals we can normally go through it and clearly highlight the parts that are God and the ones that are not.

How can we be so sure, you say? It is because we know His voice. We hear His voice all the time. I know what He sounds like. I am in a relationship with Him. When you are in a relationship with somebody and intimate with them, you know what they think and what they will say.

The Key to Judging Other Prophets

Couple that with your knowledge of the word and you have such a foundation that will enable you to judge other prophets. It gives you the wisdom and the spiritual discernment to be able to see what is of God and what is not.

Do you want to understand deception and avoid it? If you want to be able to identify what is of God and what is not in your life, this right here is the key!

Entering into that face-to-face relationship with the Lord Jesus is like the key that opens the door to your whole prophetic walk! Right here you reach a new level of spirituality. You break through the plateau.

You are going way beyond what you have known and what you have understood so far. You are going way beyond works here. You are going to the level that you always dreamt about but never quite got to.

You have been trying to go around the mountain, up and down the mountain but have actually held the key in your hand all along. All you have to do is coming to a relationship with Jesus. This is a vital part of your prophetic training! Without this phase you are not reaching the end.

How About That Honeymoon Now?

Perhaps for a time you might feel that you are out in the middle of nowhere. Well, there is a reason couples go on honeymoon... It is so that they can be alone and that is exactly what you need with the Lord.

When you come to that place of knowing Him, everything becomes more natural. It would be much like my husband and I walking down the street and then we meet somebody that I haven't seen in a while and that he hasn't met yet. I say, "Hey Lovey, this is an old friend of mine... "

I say to my old friend, "And this is my husband Craig!"

How hard is that? When I am in love with my husband it is so easy for me to shine and to express that love outwards so that people from all over can see it. They look at us and say, "Wow. I wish I could have a relationship like you guys have."

Well, imagine if you had a relationship like that with the Lord. You are walking along and you meet an old friend of yours. It doesn't matter whether they are a believer or not. You meet them and say, "Hey, have you met my friend Jesus?"

You are so passionate about Him and He is so real to you, it really is no problem. He is such a vital part of your life they can't help but see the excitement and joy in you. You know, that is the gospel. That is the good news! It's what they need and are hungry for.

Become an Example so Change Can Come

You might say, "Well, I don't know what's wrong with the Church. They are just happy to settle for second best. There they are just sitting in Church and it is so dead… there is no anointing, there is no anything… and they are just happy to sit there and be content with it."

Well, things are like this because that is all they know and see.

So tell me, what are you showing them that's different? First you have to shake them up out of their complacency and then when you shook them out of that you can show them the way.

However, until you have this passion and relationship in your life, what can you show them? Perhaps you can offer another bunch of principles, rules and regulations?

What do you have in your life that is real and that flows out of you? When they meet you, your passion for the Lord should bubble up and it should be so tangible that they look at you and want what you have! They must see you and want a relationship just like that with the Lord.

They will say, "I never knew there was more… I thought this was it!" They are content with what they have because they thought that this was all there is to life.

You have to show them that there is more to life! You will show them that by having a greater life in you first!

This means going through some changes yourself first. It means being able to let go of "you" and having the courage to point to Jesus.

Don't focus on yourself all the time and constantly concern yourself with "your" gifts and "your" prophetic call.

When someone constantly asks, "Did you see my new house and my new car? "

"Who cares? Ok so you got the shiniest car in town. I saw it already. So what? How does this benefit me?"

"Now give me such a car… now we have something to talk about!"

Honestly put, nobody cares what great gifts and abilities you have. They might admire you and think that you are great but they really don't care. They are more interested in how the Lord wants to bless them.

Give Me What You Have – Pretty Please?

So show them Jesus. Show them your passion for Him and that there is more to life. They will start to care! They will start to hunger. They will start to want it and ask you for it. In fact, they will start to beg you for it.

When that starts taking place, you are well on your way to bringing maturity to the body of Christ.

What are you bragging about? Is it how many times you can prophesy, how many visions you get and how often you can pray and read the word?

Or is it that you are just shining with the glow that a newly married couple has? Do you shine with the love that you feel for the Lord so much that they look at you and say,

"Ah man! I remember that first love... how do I get it back again"?

When people start saying that, you are doing something to mature the body of Christ.

What Stands Between You and Intimacy

I understand that it is not always easy. Things stand in the way. I know that much of your great big talk is just to cover up something that is inside of you.

However, you know it is time to look at this now. It is time to ask yourself honestly why you aren't in this kind of relationship with the Lord yet. It's time to look in the mirror and resolve to change!

1. The Bad Father Relationship

One of the main things that can stand between you and that door is a bad father relationship. If you had a father who didn't have that love, then it is hard to approach God the father and to come into that tender relationship with Him.

This is why it is important for you to approach the Lord Jesus, because He was both, God and man. He is easy to approach and He is there for you.

On your part it will mean taking up the challenge and actually facing those veils that have come between you and the Lord. It is not good enough any longer to just pretend that they are not there.

Something that really frustrates me, are people who make up a doctrine all around their experience.

"God doesn't heal today."

Do you know why most people who teach that say that? It is because they believed God for healing but didn't receive it! So therefore, "God doesn't heal today."

Their doctrine is based on experience and so everybody must believe it. They say, "Ah, you know that relationship is not for me. I can't enter into it."

Well, maybe it is all just because there are too many things standing in the way that you are not prepared to look at.

You are not prepared to look at your bad father relationship and the hurts of the past. You are not prepared to look at your bitterness or your fears and failures.

These are things that stand in the way, but are actually so easy to deal with. They look like such a mountain in front of you, but if you just took the time to look at them, you would be amazed at how quickly you can deal with them.

2. Wrong Teaching

Also wrong teaching can block your way to the Lord. So many preachers present the father as this big, austere, scary God who is ready to judge you any minute and is ready to wipe you out.

If you have been brought up with a lot of legalistic teaching, you are likely having a really tough time with trying to come into the presence of the Lord and trying to develop that gentle, loving relationship with Him.

If the only picture you have of the Lord is this scary, big image, then it is hard to come and enter into this relationship! It is not so easy and you will have to overcome.

3. Working Instead of Resting

Some people overemphasize the gifts as opposed to the love relationship with Jesus.

The prophets who struggle with this have a problem to be transparent and open their hearts.

They constantly work to cover up the fact that they don't have that tender relationship with the Lord. They can't just sit in His presence, bask in the anointing and just be with Him. As a result, they try and cover it up with all these works and gifts.

They are like our Michael Jackson wannabe trying to get the attention they crave, but not realizing that God will give them all they need in the peace of His presence. It is only in the quiet – in the calm of the storm that you will find the power you are looking for.

The relationship is not found at the traffic lights – it is found in the secret place. The best part about the secret place is not that you have to impress the lover of your soul – but rather that you can rest in His arms.

Maturity Accomplished: Knowing With the Spirit

When you come to the place of knowing the Lord in this intimate way, you will know with the spirit. You won't have to sit and get revelation all the time.

Imagine that my husband and I are walking down the road. I tell him what time I need to be home by and I ask him about what he thinks we should do first. Then he says, "I think we should go over here first and then we can go over there and head back home."

He gives me simple direction and it is the same with the Lord. Perhaps you are faced with a decision that you really need to make and so you just come to Him and ask. Then you will hear Him say in your spirit, "Let's go over here, let's do that and then do this!"

You won't have to sit and try and get revelation. You will just know with the spirit.

You might meet somebody and you will feel the Lord saying, "Hey, I want you to minister to this person. I want you to say this..."

It's not a big deal and there are no flashing lights! It is just simple and you know with your spirit. You get the word of knowledge and will feel the Lord right there. It just bubbles up out of you.

Now this is something to look forward to as a prophet. If you are not there yet though, it's okay. I won't put that pressure on you. You need to work through the gifts. You need to flow more in visions and urim and thummim (I teach on this more in *Practical Prophetic Ministry*). God will always continue to use you with the gifts.

He will continue to use you in that but the point is that there is more! There is a greater way of maturity and it is the most exciting walk that you can imagine as a prophet!

In conclusion, as you reach out to the Lord for this relationship, things are going to take off like never before! You will get so excited about the life you find in the Lord, that you will rise up and share it with the whole Church!

Welcome to Your Wedding

Chapter 05 – Welcome to Your Wedding

Rehearsals Are Not Such a Bad Idea After All…

I always thought that wedding rehearsals were really stupid. What's so difficult about walking down the aisle? You walk down the aisle, you say, "I do" and you live happily ever after… right?

Well, I thought that until it was my turn to walk down the aisle. I discovered that learning things like the bridal march and organizing all the wedding arrangements was not as easy as it looked in the movies.

I was very grateful for the wedding rehearsal that helped me get all of this together. It just looked so natural the way they did it on TV.

That is until you are the one in the white dress, trying not to trip over the high-heels you bought for the special occasion, but really should have worn in before the "big day" so that you did not half kill yourself as you wobbled to the front.

I learned that with the bridal march, the key is not to run down the aisle as it probably would have been my tendency to do. This little tip alone saved my neck and the peace of mind of those I walked by.

The idea is to take it nice and slow, a step at a time - giving everybody the opportunity to look at your dress as you smile sweetly. Also, keeping your hand steady is important so that you don't shake the poor bouquet out of its wrapping, because you are so nervous. All of this takes a little bit of practice.

Just like you have to learn the bridal march, in the prophetic realm, you have to learn to enter into that secret place with the Lord. In the last Chapter I challenged you to come into that face-to-face relationship with Jesus. It sounds so great and easy, but what do you really have to do to enter into it?

It Takes a Bit of Practice

How do we get from this end of the aisle to the altar and make this a done deal? It takes a little bit of practice. This is why you are reading this so that I can show you how to walk down the aisle and what to say when you get there.

So if you fell a little bit out of depth, if you feel like you are not sure what to do next, it is perfectly okay. You don't start out with the knowledge. You know, a baby is not born and knows immediately how to do the bridal march.

You don't just start out with the knowledge of how to have a relationship with the Lord. It takes a little bit of time. That's why you need to study the Word a bit and certainly having a prophetic mentor also helps.

If you didn't get it naturally, you are not abnormal. I didn't get it that way either. I didn't know that you could just naturally enter into a relationship with the Lord.

The main reason why it is not natural is because of all the hang-ups we have in life.

For my kids on the other hand, it is natural because they never knew anything else. They grew up in the knowledge of the Lord since day dot.

However, if you didn't grow up in a Christian home where you knew the Lord from the very beginning, it's not natural.

Depending on what your parents taught you, Chances are that even if you did grow up in church, it's not natural for you to know how to enter into a relationship with the Lord Jesus.

Just like it is not natural to just know what to do on the wedding night, or what to do at the wedding ceremony, it's not natural to just know what you need to do when you want to enter into an intimate relationship with the Lord.

That is why we have parents, mentors and spiritual parents. If you are at a point right now where you know that you need to enter into this relationship with the Lord but feel stuck, don't feel stressed.

This is what we will look at in this chapter. I will give you some very simple tips on taking those first few steps down the aisle towards the altar where your heavenly groom is waiting eagerly for you to enter into that relationship.

A Time of Separation Awaits You

The first thing you need to realize is that you will be called into a time of separation. You can't develop a relationship in a noisy environment. Even as a newly married couple you need to go away for a season to spend some time just to really get to know one another.

It's one thing when you are dating. You go to visit one another's houses, you go out together, you go to group socials and church meetings together and it seems that you live at one another's houses.

If you are anything like Craig and I, you are with one another until the birds start singing before you tear yourselves apart - only to be together again the next day. You think to yourself that you could live with this person forever...

That is until you marry and you move into your first home together. Then you realize, "I knew this person, but there are a couple of things that I really didn't know about them yet."

When you have that first year of married life and you live together for the first time day in and day out without anybody else around, only then can you really say that you know each other. You come to experience each other at a whole new level.

Well, it is the same with the Lord. You have come to know Him in your prayer times, in your church meetings and times of intercession. This was a great start. Sure, you have come to know Him through all that but now it is time to enter into a time of separation.

First Sign That You Are Growing Up

And so, the first thing the Lord is going to take you through in your training is that He will separate you from all the noise. You might find your ministry opportunities starting to die.

If this has happened to you and suddenly you are without church, without friends and family, don't panic, okay? You are in a good place. The Lord is just drawing you to Himself so that it's just you and Him and so you can enter into that intimate relationship.

You know, you can't develop intimacy with somebody while there is a room full of people. It's just not the same. You can't really get intimate and serious and share your heart with somebody when there are thousands of people around listening to you.

It's the same in ministry. You can't come into that intimacy with the Lord if you are so busy running around and working for Him, handling people and doing stuff.

That is realty the price you will have to pay. A lot of prophets fear this because they like it! They like the activity and they like to be needed.

To a certain extent it is normal because it is what burns in you. However, you will have to decide if you really want to enter into this relationship with the Lord and put all the noise away, or if you rather want to run after the recognition and have everybody think you are great!

If you want to go to that new level that I have spoken about already, it will mean coming into His silence and rest. It's okay if you suddenly seem to be alone. It's okay if you're not ministering like you used to.

Perhaps you felt like you were at the height of it all and things were busy, but suddenly everything died and came crashing down. You wonder what happened... Well, you just moved into your lover's nest.

It is time that you get to know the Lord now. At first, you might kick and scream a little bit and have a bit of a fuss, but by the end of it I promise you, you will look back on this time and miss it so much! You will look back and see how much you grew. You will look back on the intimacy you had with the Lord and how special it was to you and so you will miss this time.

So a word of advice - take advantage of it as much as you can. Enjoy it as much as you can. Enjoy the peace and the quiet because soon (sooner than you would like), things will be noisy again. Then you will just be longing for that quiet time with the Lord again.

You just need to ask yourself, "Do I want what God wants, or do I just want to get the recognition?" Because it is right here that your need for acceptance and recognition will be tested.

Now, I am not saying that there is anything wrong with having a need for acceptance and recognition. God has built it into us as humans. It is what gets us up in the morning. However, the key is to get those needs met in the Lord and not in what other people are saying about you.

When you come to the place of having that rest and having that need met in Him, it doesn't matter what they say about you. It doesn't matter whether they accept your word or not. You can say it straight, you can say it strong and you can say it with conviction.

You don't care what people say because you know you are speaking for God. If you desire to come to that place of security, it starts in your secret place with the Lord.

Seven Steps of Entering the Secret Place

Chapter 06 – Seven Steps of Entering the Secret Place

So let's look at just seven quick steps of how you can come into that secret place with the Lord.

Step 1 - Journaling

We have already covered this in more detail in *The Way of Dreams and Visions* so I will not go into a ton of detail here.

This is a very good place to start. Start getting used to the sound of His voice. Start getting used to flowing up out of your spirit. As you do that you start to become familiar with the Lord.

It is just like when you start dating. You start getting used to Him knowing what He does and doesn't sound like. Journaling is the best way to get you started.

If you are feeling a little dry, speak in tongues for a little bit and then do some journaling. This will help you get a flow in your spirit.

Step 2 - Practicing His Presence

This is definitely one of my absolute favorite ways of coming into the secret place. It is a powerful project.

Practicing His presence simply put is just being aware of the Lord 24 hours a day if possible. It's like going shopping with a good friend or with your spouse. You are walking along and you see something in a window and you say, "Oh wow, look at that. Isn't that interesting?"

You talk to them all the time. You are aware of them being next to you. I mean, nobody is so rude to just focus on doing their own job and never speak to the friend they are going out with.

The object of going out together is not so you can do your own thing and your friend can do theirs. Well... I sure hope you are not like that. I wouldn't want to go shopping with you if you were...

When you go out with somebody you are usually expressing your thoughts. You tell them where you want to go, when you are hungry and so on. You are aware of their presence, aren't you? Well, next time you go somewhere or do something, just take the Lord along.

While you go along your merry way and think of something, just talk to the Lord. Just tell the Lord that exact thought. For example, say, "Wow Lord, I am really hungry now!"

Does that seem too simplistic and naturalistic? Perhaps so, but you know what, the Lord is a very natural and real person and until you start treating Him as such, you won't enter into that relationship with Him.

While you still think that He is "way up there" and you have to shoot your prayers up into the sky, you won't enter into that relationship with Him.

So let's bring it down to the natural. Let's bring it down to your daily life and let's practice His presence. There is a power in just being aware of Him being with you, whether you are just driving in your car, making breakfast or going to work. It doesn't matter what you are doing - be aware of His presence.

Be aware that He is there with you 24 hours a day. When you wake up in the middle of the night with a bad dream, when you wake up in the morning and before you go to bed at night, talk to the Lord.

Treat Him like a real person and He will become a real person in your life because you will change your focus. As you see Him for whom He really is, you will know, as you are known. You will slowly start to come into intimacy until it is not just words or just an effort anymore but you really do feel Him there.

You will not have to make an effort anymore to communicate with Him because it will bubble up out of you all the time. His presence will become so real to you that He is as real as anybody else out there.

This will help you start to flow in a way that you have never flown in before. This should be a way of life for every prophet. Practice His presence.

Step 3 - Involve Him in All Parts of Your Life

So many Christians make a terrible mistake. They think that when it comes to matters of ministry and their spiritual life, they involve the Lord. The rest of their natural lives they handle themselves. Well that is until they face a crisis and don't know what to do next. The rest of the time they just do things their way.

For example, "Should I leave my job? I am afraid though because if I leave, the chances are that I might not find a better one... but I might. Only the Lord really knows... So let me ask the Lord."

However, then somebody else gives you an offer that looks good, you don't bother asking the Lord you just go ahead and do it. When you feel safe and secure, suddenly they don't need the Lord's advice...

You say, "Let's just go and get a bigger house, let's get a better car..." In all that, not once do you involve the Lord.

The attitude is, "It's obvious... I take care of my business but then when it comes to church, ministry and my spiritual life, I will involve the Lord. Unless of course I hit a financial crisis and then I cry to the Lord pitifully until He meets my need..."

How about also sharing the good and exciting things with the Lord as well? Tell Him, "Hey Lord, I am throwing a birthday party..."

"I am going to a party, want to come with me?"

That is the way it should be. Don't make the mistake that others do of excluding the Lord out of the best parts of your life. When you do that, you will start to see that you are slowly entering more and more into His presence. You are entering into such a new realm that you can't begin to imagine.

So, include Him in every part of your life!

Step 4 - Step Away From the Noise!

You can't hear the Lord while it's noisy around you. Whenever I think of the secret place I have a couple of pictures I see. One of them I share in the Journey of Tamar, my allegorical story of the prophetic journey.

There I envision the secret place as this beautiful big tree next to a river with a lovely green meadow. Here it is quiet. It is just the Lord and me and I can feel the breeze, smell the fresh grass, hear the birds in the distance... it's so silent!

Perhaps you see another picture. Perhaps you see one of those old bridal chambers with a big bed, candlelight and these big fur rugs on the floor with heavy drapes on the windows. In any case, you see it's quiet there. There is no noise.

We don't have a big marching band walking through the secret place. Call me old fashioned, but that is not my idea of romance or intimacy!

You can't come into a relationship with the Lord when there is noise in your life. Now that noise may be bitterness; it may be that there is so much ministry to do that you are constantly running around. The noise may be all your responsibilities and cares. It may be all your problems that you keep bombarding the Lord with all the time.

Get away from the noise. Learn to just come into His presence and "be". Wherever you are right now, the Lord is sitting right next to you. Feel His presence and peace. It is nice and quiet.

When you sit in His presence, you will hear His voice. If you can't hear His voice you will at least be able to sense Him there with you. So don't get stressed.

In fact, after reading this, if you have the opportunity, I want you to just sit with Him quietly before you even tackle all the things I taught you here. I want you to just sit there and be aware of Him being there with you and say, "Thank you Lord. I love you Jesus!"

Then just close your eyes and hear that breeze and take a deep breath. Don't beg Him or nag Him... just be quiet. Make a habit of it. When you are having your times of prayer, when you are getting into the Word - how much time do you take to just be quiet with Him? How much time do you spend to just get away from the noise and let Him speak to you?

Step 5 – Don't Take Any Steps Without His Direction

For a prophet this is a tough one. I tell you that right now because we have this habit - we are violent, crazy pendulum swingers!

When something looks good we are there! You are running, jumping and are so exited!

You go from one experience to the next. You go from,

"I just feel in resurrection right now! I could take on the world and the hordes of hell!"

Until you hit the other side of the pendulum with, "I cannot take this pressure any more. I am so tired of the death. No one will ever listen to me and my life will never come right… "

From heights of elation to stressed and depressed – that about sums the prophet up, on a good day.

From wanting to change the church universally you swing to not feeling like going to church and ministering to anybody. I know this problem well, but you have to work past this, okay?

Come to the place where you don't take any steps without His direction. Learn to hear His voice no matter which direction you are taking. Whether it's in your personal life, church or your ministry, learn to hear His voice. Don't just go running off. Hear Him speak to you first.

I hear so many people saying, "Okay, I am going to do this, and I will leave this ministry and start this one..." I say to them, "What did God tell you?"

They reply, "Oh, I didn't ask Him yet!"

People talk about their great plans all the time of what is happening in their lives and ministries and what they are going to do, but which one of them was really what the Lord told them?

They might say, "Well, I haven't really journaled about it yet, but I felt good in my spirit."

"Feel good where – in your spirit or in your emotions?"

That is what I usually say to them. What did God say for you to do? Did He tell you to have that person over for ministry? Did He tell you to take this step at your work or with your house? Did you get His direction?

Of course you can receive His direction in many different ways like we teach in the seven ways of hearing His voice, but did you really stop to get His direction clearly?

As a prophet, you cannot afford any "I thought this was a good idea" moments! As a prophet you only have one choice and that is to get direction and doing things God's way.

Step 6 - Journal Out Loud!

This is also a really fun project and something you should start incorporating into your prayer times as soon as you are comfortable with journaling. Journaling out loud makes the voice of the Lord so much more real!

When you journal out loud, the Lord is right there with you, even if you hear the sound of your own voice. So as you have gotten used to journaling and are comfortable with it, go someplace where there is no noise, and try speaking your journal out loud instead of writing it down.

It is such a fun way to get closer to the Lord. I don't know about you, but every time I practice just that part of coming into the secret place, I feel a fresh wind of anointing hitting me!

Journaling in song is also exciting! I am such an expressive - I like to shake it up sometimes. I get bored with the same old way of coming to the Lord. (I am no different in my marriage, but thank the Lord that my husband has developed the fruit of the spirit called longsuffering!)

I like to take my guitar and I will journal while playing. I love it. It makes me feel such a fresh anointing!

Never make your relationship with the Lord humdrum and boring. Shake it up a little! Journal out loud or sing your journals and just have fun with it! No matter what you do, just keep your presence in your life in any way possible.

Step 7 - Hear His Voice in the Word

When you are reading the Scriptures, pretend that the Lord is sitting right there with you, speaking the words to you. This may just be a slightly different way of looking at it but you will be amazed at how it changes things.

When you see the Lord sitting there speaking those words to you, you will be amazed at the revelation and what you hear Him say to you. You will be amazed at the sudden rhema that will come into your spirit. This is especially important when you are seeking the Lord for something and you feel dry in your spirit.

Let's say you have been putting out your faith for a desire. Next time you pick up the Word, do yourself a favor and don't just read. Imagine that the Lord is sitting right there next to you dictating the Word to you and speaking those very words to you right there and then! It will make the Word come to life.

It's incredible when you do that. Suddenly the Word isn't just words on a page, it isn't just logos anymore instead it is real life rhema. For the first time you will start hearing God in the Scriptures. When that happens, it's like taking big solid chunks of stone and embedding them in your spiritual foundation.

Problem Remembering the Word?

If you have a problem remembering the Word, this is the way to do it! You have to make it personal. You have to realize that it is the Lord speaking those words to you.

After all that is what it is for. It's His love book to you. It's His poetry to you, His Bride. When you read it, always take it personally and it will start to sink into your spirit and you will start realizing that the Lord has actually been speaking to you all along.

You will start to understand His character better. That is what I love especially when reading through the Psalms, the prophets or the stories of King David.

You see how He handled situations and start understanding His nature better. Even when you read about Jesus in the New Testament, you get a better feel of how He spoke to people.

When you envision Him speaking those things to you, you get a feel for the kind of person He is. He becomes so real. He becomes just like somebody you love. You don't look at the Scriptures as just words on a page anymore but see it as something He is saying to you right now.

Change your perspective and make the Word a real living thing. When you do that and put it in your spirit, it gives you such power. Then next time you get up to minister, prophesy or share anything, it will come out with such power and conviction. It helps you know that this is really the voice of God and you just want to speak it out so that everybody can hear it.

Final Phase of Training

Your prophetic training is not finished without this phase. I have given you seven very simple steps here. You can apply them all, but perhaps just one or two of them struck home to you.

You can pick just one, it doesn't matter. See which burns in you the most and start developing that relationship. Learn the bridal walk. Just make an effort to get into His presence. Get into the secret place. It will set you apart from everybody else!

Really, when I am looking at prophets and I want to see who's a mature prophet this is what I am looking for. I want to see, if this person knows the secret place. I want to know if they know how to enter into intimacy with the Lord.

The Lord showed me a lovely picture when I was going through this myself. He showed me how I came out of the darkness and I came into this little chamber where it was just Him and me. There He gave me this candle of light and it was such an intimate atmosphere. It was so quiet. This candle then started to spread light until I was completely covered in it.

When it was spread all over He said to me, "Okay, it's time for you to go now."

Then I stepped out into the darkness but I was still covered in His light. I had Him with me. That is really what this is about.

As you come into a relationship with the Lord, you will get charged and filled up with His anointing! When the time is done, then it will be your turn to go out there again. You won't go out the same way you came in though. You will go out charged up with His anointing! You will take His very presence and spirit with you.

You will find that you don't have to try so hard anymore. Everything won't be such an effort anymore. To prophecy or to share in love with somebody, to let go of bitterness and deal with the flesh – none of it will be such a fight any more.

Secret Shortcut to Prophetic Office

This is your shortcut to prophetic maturity. If ever there was one this is it! It is a shortcut to dealing with the flesh, your failures, the past, your lack of anointing… everything! This love relationship with the Lord is the way! When you are there it displaces the junk and the dross that you have inside. It undoes all the damage and it fills you up with power!

When you are done, you will go out from His presence and you will take some of that power with you. The point is that it will be so effortless and natural. People will just want to come to you to touch the hem of your garment like they did with Jesus.

Jesus was full of this. He did it all the time. He was always in the presence of the father. When He came out He glowed.

Is that not what they saw on the mount of transfiguration? He glowed with the presence of the Father. It is also what happened to Moses when he went up the mountain - he glowed.

So you have to have that time of separation. You have to be up on the mountain to sneak away secretly just you and Him face-to-face until you are so filled up. Don't be in such a hurry to get out. Wait until you are filled up until you are saturated and overflowing.

Then when God opens the door, you will be ready to step through it and ready to pour out everything that you have received during that time.

As you put all of this into practice, I want you to start speaking to those around you in the same way the Lord speaks to you. As you do that, you will take the secret place with you and introduce the Church into it as well!

Aerobics Workout for Prophets

Chapter 07 – Aerobics Workout for Prophets

Prophetic preparation is tough. You just need to read chapters 14-16 in the *Practical Prophetic Ministry* book to know that or you need to just live it a little. It's not easy, but I want to give hope to you in this chapter, because there is a secret way out.

Even though this is one of the most difficult times in the life of a prophet, there is a back door. So, in this chapter I will give you the secret to getting through that terrible, grinding, death-crushing preparation as quickly as possible.

When I was a teenager, I thought it would be a fantastic idea to start working out at the gym. You know how it was in the 80s. Everyone who was anyone was hitting the gym!

Not "getting it" yet that I was a prophet and would never be normal, tried anyway to go with the crowd and try to fit in.

So I got in there and actually discovered that I quite enjoyed going to the gym. There was nothing like waking up the next morning with terribly sore muscles, to feel that I had accomplished something the day before.

Perhaps that sounds a little whacked out to some people but for me it was normal. If I didn't have a little bit of an ache and pain, I didn't feel like I pushed myself hard enough. (And so there is the prophet popping up her head… always so dramatic!)

Now when I was working out at the gym, pushing my muscles to the limit until I ached, I never sat and complained, "Man, why does it have to be so tough? Ah this is such a terrible experience."

No, when you are at the gym and you are working out, you are always keeping the benefits in the front of your mind.

You think of how good you will look in that certain outfit by the end of the year. It is because you have that picture in your mind, that you don't complain about how tough it is. In fact, you actually embrace the pain.

Like I said… perhaps a bit crazy to everyone else, but a perfectly normal outlook for a prophet!

Bring It On Baby!

Well, that is a lot like prophetic preparation. Nobody wants to hurt. Nobody says, "Oh, yeah, come on and let's die already!"

Well, that is unless you are a prophet of course. Only prophets are crazy enough to think that this whole dying thing is fun.

You know why? It is because we know that at the end of this road there is a reason for all this pain. There is a reason for going through the deaths and travail.

There is an Easy Way Through the Drama

However, you can do this the easy way. There was a time when I was working out at the gym when I met somebody who worked there on a full-time basis that could help me out a bit with my routine.

I found that so beneficial, because I was so ignorant when it came to the use of all the different machines and routines. I didn't have a clue what I was doing. So he could take me through all the different stations to show me how I to use each machine and what I should be doing. He showed me which machines were good for me to use and which ones weren't.

For example, I am not going to bench press... can you see me doing that? You must know I was a really skinny, little thing when I was a teenager. So can you see me doing bench pressing? I don't think so. (Not that it stopped me from trying mind you...)

So he showed me what to stick to and what to let go of. That is exactly what I want to do for you in your prophetic training.

Let's take a look around prophetic preparation. Most importantly, let's look at the secrets that will help you get through it quickly, with a little less pain and a little more gain. Let's put a bounce in your step and send you on your way to prophetic training.

The points will cover in this chapter will change and transform the way you have been walking on your prophetic road so far. So please take careful note, okay?

Preparation – A Three Step Process

Preparation doesn't have to take forever. In fact, if you follow my three step process, you will shoot through your preparation very quickly.

Step 1. Identifying the Nails and the Thorns

What are the nails and the thorns? When they put Jesus on the cross, they put the nails in His hands and the thorns on His head.

So, what are the nails and the thorns you are experiencing? It is actually very simple to identify. Just think back over the last couple of days. Think about that that horrible situation or that horrible, annoying person that seemed to just rub you up the wrong way. Perhaps there was a pastor, leader or boss that picked on you so unfairly...

Your Goading Pricks

This sure sounds like a nail and a thorn to me! It is something that pricks you - something that causes you to flinch and cry out in pain. It is something that hurts your flesh, your pride and your feelings.

A good prick sounds like this: "Why is it that I face rejection and attacks everywhere I go?"

Are you getting it yet? Hello... there is a reason that you keep getting jabbed in the ribs! It's called prophetic preparation and if you want to get through it quickly, instead of fighting through those circumstances, you need to begin identifying them!

Woe is Me...

Instead of just saying, "Man, I really have it tough in life. It's just not fair. Everybody is always picking on me. It doesn't matter what church or job I go to everybody is always picking on me!"

You take on board a little persecution complex and walk around feeling sorry for yourself. No! That's like going to the gym and saying, "Man, I just don't know what this is... Every time I go to the gym my muscles ache. It's just not fair. I am sure other people have it easier."

Well, it would be a little silly to say that, wouldn't it? It is the same with your prophetic preparation. Let me tell you, people are ever so ready to be used as a thorn and a nail in your life!

So, start seeing what circumstances are squeezing you right now and what circumstances are nailing you to the wall so badly that you want to scream and shout.

I never said it was going to be fair. I am talking about circumstances that are difficult and hurt you and that perhaps even make you feel depressed or crushed.

I am referring to things that are coming at you and are out of your control. Identify the nails and the thorns because God is trying to pinpoint something in your life right now.

Step 2. Admitting Your Flesh!

It's so easy when the nails and thorns are coming at you to swear at the person that's hammering them in. You say, "I know that I should respond in love. I know that this shouldn't bother me... but it does!"

If you could actually just admit that, you would be fast on your way to dealing with whatever it is that God is exposing in you.

You see, preparation is for you - It's not for them. So here is one big reality check for you - **Of course it's not fair**! Did you expect it to be fair?

If it were fair, you wouldn't be reacting like you are right now. If it was nice and pretty, you wouldn't be swearing up the storm you are right now.

If everything was wonderful and everybody was nice to you, you would never know the flesh that is inside of you. You wouldn't see the beam. However, that is the purpose of preparation - to pull out the junk that's there.

It is so easy to look at the pressures and say, "Well, that pastor really is in the flesh. That boss of mine is really being used of the enemy right now."

Let me tell you again, all of this is not fair. It's not about what they're doing or thinking. It's not about their role but it's about you!

Hello Mr. Beam!

You must look at your own beam first. If you fail on this vital step, you will never get past preparation and enter into training. This is why I am laying it on so thick!

You know how many students I have coming to me who can't understand why they are still not in prophetic office after 40 years? Well, this is why.

It is because they have a super long list of what everybody did to them. Not once did it occur to them that God was trying to get a point across.

If you keep feeling pressured in the same area and same way no matter where you go, here is the reality check - It's not them that God is trying to get a message across to, it's you!

It's your beam that you need to look at right now. So if you can just stop and look at that beam and say, "Alright. What she did was, by the Word of God, the most unrighteous thing she has ever done in her life.

I know God will strike her... BUT let's put that aside right now and let's look at why I am reacting in this way. Why is it that when somebody pushes that little, tiny button of mine, I just explode in tears and justification?"

Two Wrong Reactions

Then also ask yourself if that is the correct way to respond to this situation. You see, you can respond in two ways. You can explode and get hysterical and even preach at the poor preacher, or you could also do the other wrong thing and just hide away and say, "Well, I am just not going to respond to that. The Lord will vindicate me. The Lord will take care of me and then they will see!"

Both responses are wrong. God wants you to say, "Okay, this really makes me flinch. This really bothers me. Why does it bother me? Is it addressing a weakness in me? Is it addressing a certain strength inside of me?"

If you could just look at that, you will immediately get a handle on your preparation. Those muscles feel good because you know that you are getting closer to the goal.

So instead of always getting discouraged because of all the pressures that are coming at you, you can get encouraged and excited.

You will suddenly see the reason for it all and say to yourself, "Oh my goodness. All these years the Lord has been trying to show me that my need to be needed has to go. He tried to show me my need for acceptance, arrogance and pride. He was trying to bring my flesh to the cross."

Again, in case you didn't hear me say it before, all of this won't be fair. Don't expect the nails and the thorns from people that will understand you.

You can hope and pray that you will have a mentor that will be gracious enough to hammer a nail into you. However, most of the time it comes from those who want to tear you down.

How do you think Jesus felt? It wasn't His disciples that put the nails in His hands. It was the soldiers that put the nails in His hands. It was His own brethren, the Jews that sent Him to the cross and shouted to crucify Him.

Do you think that was fair? We are looking at somebody here who had no sin. If ever Jesus could escape His teaching on "looking at your beam" He sure could! He was completely "beamless" in every way.

Yet even the most sinless and perfect man in the world didn't sit and complain about it. Instead He said, "Father, forgive them. Lord, into your hands I commit my spirit."

He took it on because He knew that there was a goal up ahead. He knew that a resurrection and power that the world had never seen before would follow after this. And so He felt the pain and said, "Bring it on, because I know where this pain is heading to!"

If you can start adopting that attitude to the pressures and circumstances that are squishing you right now, you will bounce through these deaths so fast that you will move headlong into training!

In fact, you might end up wondering to yourself why it to you so long to get to this point.

Step 3. Learning to Die Already!

You can't die already until you have admitted your flesh. People want to just say, "Oh... that was so uncomfortable, I'll just die already!"

"Okay, so what exactly are you letting go of and dying to?"

"Oh, I am just letting go of everybody being mean to me! I let go of all the pressures."

Don't I just wish that it worked this way! Alas, it is a full three step process and you have to follow each one.

First, identify the thorns and the nails and then admit the flesh.

Admit that you have a problem. Admit that your reaction is wrong and that it hurts. Admit that this brought something out of you that is less than godly. It is a good place to be.

When you finally come to that place and see all the junk, your weakness and your natural strength that makes you want to get in there and do it all yourself, you realize that you can't actually do it.

You will say to the Lord, "Lord, I can't handle this rejection. I can't face this pressure. Lord, I see that I don't even have a tiny ounce of love in me!

I know that this person who is coming against me it is so wrong but I just don't have it in me to respond the way I should."

Good - now you are ready to die already. Now you are ready to come to the place of acknowledging that it's not fair but that it hurts and you don't know how to handle it correctly.

You might even say to the Lord, "I don't even know how to die Lord!"

It's good because now you are ready to really commit your spirit into His hands. You are now ready to really let go.

In Spite of How You Feel...

At this point you will no longer justify yourself or argue. You will also no longer struggle or try to pull love out of your toes somewhere. You come to the cross and die in spite of how you feel. You give up waiting for your feelings to change first.

You surrender to the Lord and let Him know that you will just let His love flow through you. You say, "Into your hands I commit my spirit!"

Don't you feel that deep stirring that calls you to this death? Actually, it is not a bad thing. In fact, you will feel that you can breathe properly for the first time in ages.

I have had a dream many times during my prophetic training where I was swimming under water and I was so afraid that I would drown, but then suddenly I take a breath and discover that I can breathe under water.

This is kind of like what this preparation process is like also. At first you keep fighting the death. You struggle with the flesh and the pressures come on you. The nails are hammered in and you cry out but eventually you get to a point where you just can't handle it anymore.

You realize, "Hang on a minute, I am not making it here", and so you surrender. At this point you realize that you can breathe under water!

Full Surrender

You realize that when you let go and die already, you get up on that cross and Christ gets off. That He does something in your life that you cannot. To quote a scripture, *"But when that which is perfect has come, then that which is in part will be done away." (1 Cor 13:10)*

In other words, when that pressure or circumstance has accomplished the death in you that it needed to, it will no longer be a problem. You won't have to face that death again.

If you truly die to it, you won't have to face it again. So this is your shortcut. Your shortcut is through the cross.

So be prepared to go through the cross. Have the grace to learn to die already and don't argue. Could you imagine Jesus standing there saying, "Well, look guys, the truth is, I am really innocent and I just don't think you should be nailing into me right now. Let's look at this logically."

I don't think so. The Scripture says, "Just as a sheep is silent before its shearers, so Jesus was silent."

It says that He didn't say a word to defend Himself. It says that He just took the nails. In fact, when the nails came He said, "Into your hands I commit my spirit father."

How Much Longer?

He knew something better was coming. If you find that you are just not moving on right now and that the pressures are increasing with no time left for you to breathe, leaving you with a desire to simply scream…. good.

How much longer will it be before you come to the end of yourself? How much longer before you give God control? How much longer before you get on that cross so Christ can get off?

How many more things and rejections, pressures and chisels do you have to endure before you get it? How much more must you take before you realize that it is no longer you who lives but Christ who lives in you and this life you now live in the flesh you live in Him...? (Gal 2:20)

It isn't about if you are right or wrong. It's not about what is good and what is bad. It's not about what is righteous and what is not. None of those things matter.

It is about how you are responding. It's about what God is addressing in you. If you can just admit and submit to that you got a one-way ticket to the end of this journey!

You can feel the rest, learn to breathe under water and flex your muscles – with a new strength and power you never had before.

As you start going through all these teachings, you will start feeling the call to death. Not in a bad way, but in a positive one. You will experience some good death to the flesh coming on you.

There are many out there who say, "Oh, God is calling me to death", but do they ever really "die already"?

Often people say, "I am going through a death right now!"

What they are saying in other words is that they are kicking up on the cross, squealing like a pig so that their legs have to be broken. That is not learning to die already!

When do you really come to the place of submitting your flesh to the cross and letting Christ be in control?

Prophetic Landmarks

Chapter 08 – Prophetic Landmarks

I have an unmistakable flaw in that I could get lost in my own backyard. My sense of direction is horrible to the point that my husband has a joke. He says to me, "Love, whenever you feel totally confident that you must take the right hand turn, do a full 180 and go to the left because the chances are you are wrong!"

We call it the "Toach rule". He would always say, "Babe, when you want to take a turn, the Toach rule applies."

We would go shopping in a mall that we have been to many times and we would go ahead to the parking lot. So I head out the door and I am convinced we have to go to the right and then my husband would give me that look and say, "Lovey, once again, 'Toach rule' applies!" I stand there realizing that once again I am going in the completely wrong direction.

Well, he made more trouble for himself because my husband was also the one to teach me how to drive.

And so here we have this lovely combination of learning how to drive and not getting lost! He had quite a case on his hands but he gave me a really wonderful pointer.

He said, "You know, when you are going anywhere, take note of the landmarks around you. Then, before you even head out on a journey, close your eyes and see where you will go, what turn offs you will take and what method of attack you will use to go on this journey."

If you already have a picture of the landmarks in your mind and can see that half torn down pole at one intersection, the gas station on the left over there and remember the bright pink building on the right... you will know where you need to go.

You won't have to remember things like, "At the first light, turn to the right".

Don't you hate people that give you that kind of direction? They say, "Just go down three intersections and then take a left by the stop street until the third set of traffic lights and then take the second...."

I never remember those kinds of instructions. So my husband gave me the easy way out and told me to look out for landmarks.

And so before I head out on any journey, I can immediately run through the direction I am going quickly in my mind, pinpointing the main places where I will change direction.

The Three Landmarks in Your Prophetic Preparation

Well, I want to look at some of those milestones in your prophetic preparation. There are three very clear landmarks that you need to identify before you head out.

Those three landmarks are death, resurrection and glorification.

If you can identify those landmarks before you head out – you are less likely to hit the wall,

Don't just head out there into the great unknown not knowing where you are going. Have a little bit of hindsight.

So let's look at these three landmarks in more detail because you will face them again and again through your prophetic preparation - not only that but right through your training also. Actually, not only that, you will face this even when you are in prophetic office.

So memorize these and learn to live with them. Learn to see them, smell them, touch, taste and hear them. You can be sure that you will always be heading in the right direction when you do that.

1. Death

What is the horrible process of death to the flesh really about? How do you identify this process?

Well, firstly, your weaknesses are exposed. Sin is exposed and also your strength is exposed. You see all the flaws and the things that must change. This is a phase that you will experience again and again. Just look back over the last couple of months in your life – the last year – and you will be able to pinpoint this landmark in your life many times.

I am speaking about situations that you faced where all the junk came out and your sin was exposed - where you felt so horrible and depressed, discouraged, rejected and denounced…

So all this stuff comes up and you see all these flaws and problems… BUT that's not death. It is just the precursor. It is just the warning sign that says, "You need to take this turn here."

Death only comes when you see your sin and you come to the place of realizing that you cannot fix yourself.

You cannot say that you have been through the process of death until you have really learned to die already! You see - the pressures and difficult situations aren't the death.

Death means coming to the point of realizing that you can't do it. Death means seeing your sin and realizing that you cannot save yourself but need a savior.

Death is coming to the point of realizing that you can't even do what God wants you to do – that you can't even desire what He wants you to desire.

You try to walk in the spirit and all this flesh comes up so that all you see is sin. Death is not seeing your sin and then trying to fix it.

"Well, I see that I have sin in this area so I am just going to stop sinning and therefore I have learned to die already!"

Oh no… you haven't even reached the first landmark yet - that is not death. You can't fix the flesh with the flesh.

Death can only come when you realize that you cannot fix your flesh.

That Pesky Right Hand!

"Oh wretched man that I am who will deliver me from this body of sin," Apostle Paul said. I sure understand this man. You want to serve God. You want to do it right and apply these principles so badly and to walk in faith, hope and love. You want to be in the spirit but... wretched man that I am!

This horrible sin keeps coming up. These thoughts keep coming to my mind and suddenly my right hand is doing what I know it shouldn't do.

You struggle and try harder. So you say, "Okay, I will just sin less. That's it! From now on I will say no to all that food that I keep eating, because I know it is sin. I know it is gluttony. I will just say no. I won't eat that chocolate cake or that donut... Oh boy... I can just see that donut..."

The next thing you know, you are giving in to the flesh! Why – it's because that is all you are thinking about. You are thinking about all the wrong things that you are doing and the flesh all the time!

Well then, guess what? You are just producing more flesh and sin because it is all you are thinking about all the time so that is what you will produce.

You know, it is just like somebody who wants to quit smoking. They say, "I will not smoke. I will not smoke!" What picture is in their mind? Smoke, cigarettes.... Them puffing on a cigarette all the time...

The worst is you will give in and feel so guilty. You sinned and failed again. You let that weakness come up again and now you feel so bad about it. Then the enemy says, "Yeah, look at you. You messed up!"

You see, you didn't die! You just identified your flesh and then tried to fix your flesh with more flesh. Well, darkness cannot take out darkness. You cannot walk into a dark room and take a bucket and throw buckets of darkness out the room. No, you just turn on the light and the darkness leaves.

When you come to that point of realizing that you cannot fix your flesh then you say, "Lord, if you can use this vessel, go for it... but I can't fix my flesh. Into your hands I commit my flesh. Forgive me father. Help me Lord. I need a savior!"

When you say that you show that you are learning to "die already" - then you switch on the light and start discovering the power of death and resurrection.

You realize that death is coming to a point when you see that you cannot stop sinning. There is something inside of you, the seed of sin in your flesh that propels you.

It is even like Apostle Paul said, "Even though I know what's right I find myself doing those things that I know I shouldn't do. Oh wretched man..."

When Will I Change?

Only when you realize that you cannot fix your flesh but that you can only yield it to the cross! However, even though you arrive at the point of giving up your flesh and letting go, change doesn't come just yet.

It just leads you to a point of being in the grave and being dead to the flesh. The change comes in our second landmark which is resurrection!

2. Resurrection

Here is a classic situation - The Lord has just exposed in you, your terrible need to always be in control. You realize that you are nothing but controlling and arrogant and that you use other people to get what you want.

You say, "Oh Lord, what kind of leader have I been? I have been a controlling, insecure leader that has pushed everybody around. I have had no love or grace!"

You feel so horrible and come to a point of realizing that you can't even have real love, compassion or tenderness and so you come to the cross and you say, "Lord, I just can't do this and I let it go! Lord, help me."

The next day, an opportunity comes and somebody knocks at your door. You have to step out there into active ministry show them compassion and love.

Another scenario - Somebody comes to you with the exact same sin and now you have to minister to them.

You are thinking, "Lord, you have got to be kidding, right? Here I just have gone through this whole death of how I can't show love and compassion and now I have to preach about that? I am such a hypocrite right now I could just crawl into a hole and die!"

By His Grace!

Those are good resurrections! They are very humbling and they bring you to a place where you say, "By His grace alone!"

When you stand up to preach you know well that there is no good thing within you. When you stand up in that resurrection and submit, you will experience the anointing in a way that you never have before.

Then you will stand up to minister or preach and you will get revelation like you never have before. You will also get such power that by the time you get down from there, God just did something in you!

You stand up there and preach on this thing and you feel this love and this compassion that you cannot help but stand in awe of what God has just done.

You know what the problem is though? The problem is you are waiting for the anointing before you step out! Just like you struggle to learn to die already, when you finally do "die already" you sit in the grave waiting for the change to come upon you before you step out.

Perhaps God has dealt with your spiritual arrogance of thinking that you are better than everybody else. Then He shows you that you are as sinful as the next guy and you feel so bad about it.

Then He opens up an opportunity for you to minister but you don't want to do it because you are waiting for the love and change to come to your heart first. You want to look in the mirror first and see the change and when you see it you will be ready to step out!

Changes Comes in Resurrection!

I am afraid it doesn't happen that way. Change comes in the resurrection! It doesn't come in the process of death. Tell me, when was the kingdom of God established? Was it when Jesus said, "It is finished" or when He resurrected and all the disciples could see Him?

It is when they saw Him resurrect in power that the New Testament Church was born. He said to them, "Receive the Holy Spirit!" It was in His resurrection that the power came and that He was changed.

It wasn't in the death. Death was just a doorway. The death just prepares you for the power that is to come but it's not the end of the process. In fact, it's just the beginning. It's a doorway to resurrection and onto glorification.

That is where the power is and that is a very exciting way.

The change comes in the resurrection! Have you been sitting in the grave and the death month after month? The change won't come there. You won't suddenly feel better!

Perhaps the Lord has brought to death your need for acceptance or for recognition. And so you are waiting for this need to just suddenly go away. You have brought it to death and you have identified it, and said, "Lord I give it up to you!"

So you are sitting there waiting until you cannot feel it anymore and you are wondering why nothing is happening. Do you know when it will change?

Start Stepping!

When you get out of your hole and start stepping. Allow God to use you and then, as you are flowing out you will do it in such weakness, because you will know what God just addressed in you. You will know the sin that's there!

It's such a humbling place to be. There you are - ministering about the exact same thing you just messed up with!

Only after that, will you realize that the need is not there anymore. The more you step out and the more you are in His anointing it's like water that flows through you. You know it comes from your spirit and it takes all the dirt away with it. It also transforms you because the same spirit that raised Christ from the dead is also in you and it will quicken your mortal body.

This is when you get past the death and you say, "Okay Lord, let me step out now and let me pour out in tremendous humility."

I usually had my greatest deaths just before a meeting. In fact, my husband can just shake his head and smile at this one, because some of the greatest death experiences we have had is in the car on the way to the meeting.

Drive-Through Crucifixion

Just peachy! God will suddenly expose something or there will be a conflict just before the meeting. Suddenly all our junk is coming up and... guess what? I have got five minutes to "die already!"

"Okay Lord, that's just great. I am about to get in there and give these people what you have given me and here you are exposing all this sin in me. That's just peachy... thanks!"

Actually, it is good when it happens like that, because then you have got nowhere to hide. This is when you really learn to die already – trust me on this one. So you cry out to the Lord, die already, wipe your face and reapply your mascara (or straighten your tie), arrive and everybody thinks you are so full of the joy of the Lord!

On your end you'd rather crawl into a hole though...
Then you stand up and all these faces are looking at you
waiting to hear what God has to say.

You look back and think, "I have nothing to give you,
because there is no good thing in me! Lord, not my will
but your will be done. If you want to use me, use me!"

I tell you, in the times when I have faced this landmark,
are the times the Lord used me in powerful ways. You
realize that it's no longer "I that lives" but Christ that
lives in me.

You really get on that cross and Jesus says to you,
"Thank you. Now I can get off!"

He is the one with the power, the glory and the
anointing. When you face such an experience you stand
in such humility. You know what's in you but then you
also know that He who is in you is greater that your sin
and flesh!

When you experience that power and overcome that
weakness that God has exposed, it is time to move on to
landmark number three.

3. Glorification

This is the best landmark of all! The Lord isn't just going
to resurrect you to where you were before. He wants to
take you higher. He wants to give you a greater vision.
He wants to give you more responsibility.

You see, that's why He brought you to death in the first place. He wanted to deal with your pride because He wanted to give you more. He wanted to deal with your need for control because He wanted to put more people under you.

He wanted you to deal with your need for acceptance so that you could reach out to more than you ever have before. You see, those stumbling blocks of the flesh have stood in your way. Your reliance on those strengths has stood in your way for the greater vision God has for you.

Higher, Faster, Stronger

So as wonderful as it is, not even resurrection is the end road here. You must step into phase three and not revert back to the grave again. You must push forward, because God wants to give you more than you had before.

If you are only working with one person, God wants you to work with two. If you were only ministering in one capacity, He wants you to minister in more than you have before. That's the purpose of it and it is the best part.

When it comes to stepping into the authority of the prophet, this is the journey you need to take. These are the landmarks you need to pass.

When you have been through the death where you are so vulnerable and stripped down before the Lord and you have been through the resurrection and you know that it is by His grace alone, God usually says to you, "Well done my good and faithful servant! Because you have taken those five talents and you have multiplied them and have been prepared to push through, here is another five.

Here is more than you ever had before. You have now proved yourself with a little so I will give you more authority and responsibility."

You will rise up that way. If you feel stuck as if you are going around in circles, then you are missing these landmarks. You are driving on the highway and you see a landmark there and you just drive right past. You are missing the road.

Don't try and skip one of these. Don't sit and wallow in the grave, but on the other hand, don't just jump to resurrection and think that you will just push through and push through… No, that doesn't help either.

The Key to Prophetic Authority

Do you want to know how to walk in prophetic authority? You have seen how I operate and if you are familiar with our ministry you have seen how all of the prophets and apostles operate. You cannot help but see the authority.

It is just like the Jews said of Jesus, "He doesn't speak like the Scribes. He speaks with authority." Of the disciples they said, "We can see they have been with Jesus, because they speak with authority!"

Well, where does that authority come from? Where does the extra "something" come from? It comes from being glorified - from going through the process of death, then resurrection and then going beyond that to taking on more than you ever have before. You take on a greater responsibility that God has for you!

So don't squeal when it comes. When there is more pressure, more people and more responsibility than you can handle then it's time to be glorified.

The great thing is that when you have really gone through the death and the resurrection process, you can take it in your stride. Those two processes prepare you for the final one.

If you really come to the place of knowing that, then God can trust you with so much more.

He knows that you won't take things out of His hands. He knows that He can take you anywhere and give you His anointing and power. He knows that you won't abuse it to manipulate people or make yourself look good.

You will use it for His benefit and so He will give you more than you ever had before. Do you want more? Do you want more power and authority?

Identify these landmarks and learn to go through this process, because God wants you to rise up in that authority but you have to prove yourself first. As you prove yourself you will rise up as a prophet that everybody will look at and say, "I can see that he has been with Jesus because of the authority he speaks with. "

The Starting Line of Your Journey

If you have taken these principles and you really made them your own through this book, you are well prepared and ready to become the prophet God has called you to be.

I can give you principles and share my personal experience. I can even tell you what God will do, but as for whether or not you will make it, that's up to you. It's not even up to the Lord.

Will you make it through prophetic training? It's really up to you. Are you really willing to pay the price? Are you really willing to do this God's way? Are you willing to face the death, to face the flesh and look at yourself? Are you prepared to step out in your own weakness but in His power?

I can only present these principles to you. I can only point out the road as you walk it but it's the Holy Spirit that brings the pressure and it's for you to say, "Father, into your hands I commit my spirit." Only you can do that. Only you can make these principles part of your life!

The question remains... What are you going to do about it? After you have learned all of this stuff and gone through all our prophetic teachings, your head is full now with so much knowledge.

What Are You Going to Do About It?

You have lived a few experiences and that's great! After all you have learned, after all the projects you have done, now what are you really going to do about it?

Is it just going to be another book you've read? Is it just going to be another bunch of teaching that you have crammed inside of your mind or is this going to be something that you will allow to change your life? I can't answer that question for you. Not even God can answer this for you. Only you can!

So before you press on, ask yourself, "Have I really given my heart into this? Am I ready to change?

Am I ready to let God do something in my heart and not just in my mind? "

Like I said, only you will ever know!

Well, this is the moment... this is the end of this book! You have survived this far and I congratulate you! Know though that this is not the end. There are more prophetic training materials we have available to you.

You can check out *Practical Prophetic Ministry* or *Prophetic Essentials* next. Your journey is only just beginning!

About the Author

Born in Bulawayo, Zimbabwe and raised in South Africa, Colette had a zeal to serve the Lord from a young age. Coming from a long line of Christian leaders and having grown up as a pastor's kid, she is no stranger to the realities of ministry. Despite having to endure many hardships such as her parent's divorce, rejection, and poverty, she continues to follow after the Lord passionately. Overcoming these obstacles early in her life has built a foundation of compassion and desire to help others gain victory in their lives.

Since then, the Lord has led Colette, with her husband Craig Toach, to establish *Apostolic Movement International,* a ministry to train and minister to Christian leaders all over the world, where they share all the wisdom that the Lord has given them through each and every time they chose to walk through the refining fire in their personal lives, as well as in ministry.

In addition, Colette is a fantastic cook, an amazing mom to not only her 4 natural children, but to her numerous spiritual children all over the world. Colette is also a renowned author, mentor, trainer and a woman that has great taste in shoes! The scripture to "be all things to all men" definitely applies here, and the Lord keeps adding to that list of things each and every day.

How does she do it all? Experience through every book and teaching the life of an apostle firsthand, and get the insight into how the call of God can make every aspect of your life an incredible adventure.

Read more at www.colette-toach.com

Connect with Colette Toach on Facebook!
www.facebook.com/ColetteToach

Check Colette out on Amazon.com at:
www.amazon.com/author/colettetoach

Recommendations by the Author

Note: All reference of AMI refers to Apostolic Movement International.

If you enjoyed this book, we know you will love the following on the prophetic.

Presentation of Prophecy

By Colette Toach

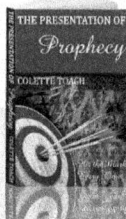

You do not need to be a prophet to prophecy and God will not come forcibly on you and make you do anything.

It is indeed a gift of the spirit that can be practiced. By the end of this book, you will be amazed to discover how accessible this gift of the Holy Spirit is to you. You will know the steps 1, 2, 3 of presenting prophecy.

Practical Prophetic Ministry

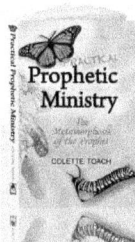

By Colette Toach

Wouldn't it be incredible if someone could have walked you through your prophetic calling and pointed out all the potholes before you fell into them?

Unfolded step by step, you will have someone along the way telling you what to avoid, what to embrace and most importantly... what to do next along your prophetic journey.

Prophetic Essentials

Book 1 of the Prophetic Field Guide Series

By Colette Toach

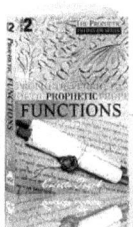

In this book, you will find out that the call of the prophet goes far deeper than the functions and duties that the prophet fulfills. Anyone flowing in prophetic ministry can carry out tasks similar to the prophet.

If it burns in you to pay any price that is necessary and to stand up and break down the barriers between the Lord Jesus and His Bride, then my friend, you have picked up the right tool that will confirm the fire in your belly and the call of God on your life.

Prophetic Functions

Book 2 of the Prophetic Field Guide Series

By Colette Toach

There is so much more to the prophet than standing up in church and prophesying.

Laid out beautifully so that you can understand and relate, Colette shares from her own personal experiences. Be prepared to live and experience the Lord like never before. This is not fiction... this is your training guide to the prophetic.

A.M.I. Prophetic School

www.prophetic-school.com

Whether you are just starting out or have been along the way for some time, we all have questions.

Who better to answer them than another prophet!

With over 18 years of experience, the A.M.I. Prophetic School is the leader in the prophetic realm.

From dedicated lecturers to live streaming and graduation, the A.M.I. Prophetic School is your home away from home.

What Our Prophetic Training Accomplishes

Our extensive training is a full two-year curriculum that will:

1. Identify and confirm your prophetic call
2. Effectively train you to flow in all the gifts of the Spirit
3. Fulfill your purpose as a prophet in the local church
4. Take your hand through the prophetic training process
5. Specialist training in spiritual warfare
6. Arm you for intercession and decree
7. Minister in praise and worship
8. Achieve prophetic maturity

Contact Information

To check out our wide selection of materials, go to:
www.ami-bookshop.com

Do you have any questions about any products?

Contact us at: +1 (760) 466 - 7679
(8am to 5pm California Time, Weekdays Only)

E-mail Address: admin@ami-bookshop.com

Postal Address:

> A.M.I.
> 5663 Balboa Ave #416
> San Diego, CA 92111, USA

Facebook Page:
http://www.facebook.com/ApostolicMovementInternational

YouTube Page:
https://www.youtube.com/c/ApostolicMovementInternational

Twitter Page: https://twitter.com/apmoveint

Amazon.com Page: www.amazon.com/author/colettetoach

AMI Bookshop – It's not Just Knowledge, It's **Living Knowledge**